HMH SCIENCE DIMENSIONS™
Volume 2

Grade 5
Units 5–7

This Write-In Book belongs to

_____

Teacher/Room

_____

Houghton Mifflin Harcourt™

Consulting Authors

Michael A. DiSpezio
Global Educator
North Falmouth, Massachusetts

Marjorie Frank
*Science Writer and Content-Area
    Reading Specialist*
Brooklyn, New York

Michael R. Heithaus, PhD
*Dean, College of Arts, Sciences &
    Education*
*Professor, Department of Biological
    Sciences*
Florida International University
Miami, Florida

Cary Sneider, PhD
Associate Research Professor
Portland State University
Portland, Oregon

Program Advisors

Paul D. Asimow, PhD
Eleanor and John R. McMillan Professor of Geology and Geochemistry
California Institute of Technology
Pasadena, California

Eileen Cashman, PhD
Professor
Humboldt State University
Arcata, California

Mark B. Moldwin, PhD
Professor of Space Sciences and Engineering
University of Michigan
Ann Arbor, Michigan

Kelly Y. Neiles, PhD
Assistant Professor of Chemistry
St. Mary's College of Maryland
St. Mary's City, Maryland

Sten Odenwald, PhD
Astronomer
NASA Goddard Spaceflight Center
Greenbelt, Maryland

Bruce W. Schafer
Director of K–12 STEM Collaborations, retired
Oregon University System
Portland, Oregon

Barry A. Van Deman
President and CEO
Museum of Life and Science
Durham, North Carolina

Kim Withers, PhD
Assistant Professor
Texas A&M University-Corpus Christi
Corpus Christi, Texas

Adam D. Woods, PhD
Professor
California State University, Fullerton
Fullerton, California

Classroom Reviewers

Michelle Barnett
Lichen K–8 School
Citrus Heights, California

Brandi Bazarnik
Skycrest Elementary
Citrus Heights, California

Kristin Wojes-Broetzmann
Saint Anthony Parish School
Menomonee Falls, Wisconsin

Andrea Brown
District Science and STEAM Curriculum TOSA
Hacienda La Puente Unified School District
Hacienda Heights, California

Denice Gayner
Earl LeGette Elementary
Fair Oaks, California

Emily Giles
Elementary Curriculum Consultant
Kenton County School District
Ft. Wright, Kentucky

Crystal Hintzman
Director of Curriculum, Instruction and Assessment
School District of Superior
Superior, Wisconsin

Roya Hosseini
Junction Avenue K–8 School
Livermore, California

Cynthia Alexander Kirk
Classroom Teacher, Learning Specialist
West Creek Academy
Valencia, California

Marie LaCross
Fair Oaks Ranch Community School
Santa Clarita, California

Emily Miller
Science Specialist
Madison Metropolitan School District
Madison, Wisconsin

Monica Murray, EdD
Principal
Bassett Unified School District
La Puente, California

Wendy Savaske
Director of Instructional Services
School District of Holmen
Holmen, Wisconsin

Tina Topoleski
District Science Supervisor
Jackson School District
Jackson, New Jersey

You are a scientist!

You are naturally curious.

Have you wondered . . .

- is ice still water?
- if you could float in midair?
- how you can talk to your friend on a cell phone?
- if plants can grow without soil?

_____

_____

_____

_____

Write in some other things you wonder about.

HMH SCIENCE DIMENSIONS™

.will **SPARK** your curiosity

AND prepare you for

√ tomorrow

√ next year

√ college or career

√ life

Where do you see yourself in 20 years?

Write in or draw another career you'd like.

Be a scientist.

Work like real scientists work.

Plan

Investiga

Have Fun

Be an engineer.

Solve problems like engineers do.

Design

Solve Problems

Share Solutions

Explain your world.

Start by asking questions.

Think Critically

Make a Claim

Gather Evidence

There's more than one way to the answer. What's YOURS?

Work in Teams

Develop Explanations

Support Your Conclusions

Engineering and Technology...... 1

Systems in Space

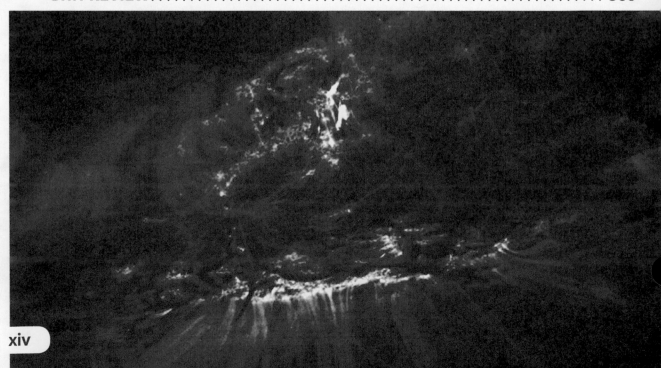

Safety in the Lab

Doing science is a lot of fun. But, a science lab can be a dangerous place. Falls, cuts, and burns can happen easily. **Know the safety rules and listen to your teacher.**

☐ **Think ahead.** Study the investigation steps so you know what to expect. If you have any questions, ask your teacher. Be sure you understand all caution statements and safety reminders.

☐ **Be neat and clean.** Keep your work area clean. If you have long hair, pull it back so it doesn't get in the way. Roll or push up long sleeves to keep them away from your activity.

☐ **Oops!** If you spill or break something, or get cut, tell your teacher right away.

☐ **Watch your eyes.** Wear safety goggles anytime you are directed to do so. If you get anything in your eyes, tell your teacher right away.

☐ **Yuck!** Never eat or drink anything during a science activity.

☐ **Don't get shocked.** Be careful if an electric appliance is used. Be sure that electric cords are in a safe place where you can't trip over them. Never use the cord to pull a plug from an outlet.

☐ **Keep it clean.** Always clean up when you have finished. Put everything away and wipe your work area. Wash your hands.

☐ **Play it safe.** Always know where to find safety equipment, such as fire extinguishers. Know how to use the safety equipment around you.

Safety in the Field

Lots of science research happens outdoors. It's fun to explore the wild! But, you need to be careful. The weather, the land, and the living things can surprise you.

☐ **Think ahead.** Study the investigation steps so you know what to expect. If you have any questions, ask your teacher. Be sure you understand all caution statements and safety reminders.

☐ **Dress right.** Wear appropriate clothes and shoes for the outdoors. Cover up and wear sunscreen and sunglasses for sun safety.

☐ **Clean up the area.** Follow your teacher's instructions for when and how to throw away waste.

☐ **Oops!** Tell your teacher right away if you break something or get hurt.

☐ **Watch your eyes.** Wear safety goggles when directed to do so. If you get anything in your eyes, tell your teacher right away.

☐ **Yuck!** Never taste anything outdoors.

☐ **Stay with your group.** Work in the area as directed by your teacher. Stay on marked trails.

☐ **"Wilderness" doesn't mean go wild.** Never engage in horseplay, games, or pranks.

☐ **Always walk.** No running!

☐ **Play it safe.** Know where safety equipment can be found and how to use it. Know how to get help.

☐ **Clean up.** Wash your hands with soap and water when you come back indoors.

Safety Symbols

To highlight important safety concerns, the following symbols are used in a Hands-On Activity. Remember that no matter what safety symbols you see, all safety rules should be followed at all times.

Dress Code

- Wear safety goggles as directed.
- If anything gets into your eye, tell your teacher immediately
- Do not wear contact lenses in the lab.
- Wear appropriate protective gloves as directed.
- Tie back long hair, secure loose clothing, and remove loose jewelry.

Glassware and Sharp Object Safety

- Do not use chipped or cracked glassware.
- Notify your teacher immediately if a piece of glass breaks.
- Use extreme care when handling all sharp and pointed instruments.
- Do not cut an object while holding the object in your hands.
- Cut objects on a suitable surface, always in a direction away from your body.

Electrical Safety

- Do not use equipment with frayed electrical cords or loose plugs.
- Do not use electrical equipment near water or when clothing or hands are wet.
- Hold the plug when you plug in or unplug equipment.

Chemical Safety

- If a chemical gets on your skin, on your clothing, or in your eyes, rinse it immediately, and tell your teacher.
- Do not clean up spilled chemicals unless your teacher directs you to do so.
- Keep your hands away from your face while you are working on any activity.

Heating and Fire Safety

- Know your school's evacuation-fire routes.
- Never leave a hot plate unattended while it is turned on or while it is cooling.
- Allow equipment to cool before storing it.

Plant and Animal Safety

- Do not eat any part of a plant.
- Do not pick any wild plant unless your teacher instructs you to do so.
- Treat animals carefully and respectfully.
- Wash your hands throughly after handling any plant or animal.

Cleanup

- Clean all work surfaces and protective equipment as directed by your teacher.
- Wash your hands throughly before you leave the lab or after any activity.

Safety Quiz

Name _____

Circle the letter of the BEST answer.

1. Before starting an activity, you should
   a. try an experiment of your own.
   b. open all containers and packages.
   c. read all directions and make sure you understand them.
   d. handle all the equipment to become familiar with it.

2. At the end of any activity, you should
   a. wash your hands thoroughly before leaving the lab.
   b. cover your face with your hands.
   c. put on your safety goggles.
   d. leave the materials where they are.

3. If you get hurt or injured in any way, you should
   a. tell your teacher immediately.
   b. find bandages or a first aid kit.
   c. go to your principal's office.
   d. get help after you finish the activity.

4. If your equipment is chipped or **broken**, you should
   a. use it only for solid materials.
   b. give it to your teacher for recycling or disposal.
   c. put it back.
   d. increase the damage so that it is obvious.

5. If you have unused liquids after finishing an activity, you should
   a. pour them down a sink or drain.
   b. mix them all together in a bucket.
   c. put them back into their original containers.
   d. dispose of them as directed by your teacher.

6. When working with materials that might fly into the air and hurt someone's eye, you should wear
   a. goggles.
   b. an apron.
   c. gloves.
   d. a hat.

7. If you get something in your eye, you should
   a. wash your hands immediately.
   b. put the lid back on the container.
   c. wait to see if your eye becomes irritated.
   d. tell your teacher right away.

Systems in Space

Explore
Online

Unit Project: Starry Sky
Can you see the same stars in the sky all year long? Investigate, and then construct a seasonal star guide with your team. Ask your teacher for details.

At a Glance

Vocabulary Game: Forbidden Words

Materials
- 1 set of word cards, with forbidden terms included, per team

How to Play
1. Work in teams of two.
2. Pair up with another team of two players.
3. Place the word cards face down on the table.
4. A player on one team picks a word card. The player with the card describes the word to the partner without using any of the forbidden terms on the card.
5. If the partner correctly determines the word, the team receives 5 points. For each forbidden word used, the team loses a point.
6. The other team then selects a card and takes a turn.
7. Repeat until all the cards have been used. The team with the most points wins the game.

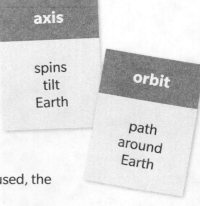

axis

spins
tilt
Earth

orbit

path
around
Earth

Unit Vocabulary

axis: The imaginary line around which Earth rotates.

constellation: A pattern of stars that forms an imaginary picture or design in the sky.

gravity: A force that pulls things toward the center of Earth.

hemisphere: One half of Earth.

orbit: The path of one object in space around another object.

revolution: The movement of Earth one time around the sun.

rotation: The turning of Earth on its axis.

How Does Gravity Affect Matter on Earth?

Earth's curved shape is easily seen from space. When standing on Earth, it is difficult to know you are living on a sphere.

By the end of this lesson . . .
you'll be able to discuss how gravity affects all matter on Earth.

Can You Explain It?

Our planet, Earth, is constantly moving. The continents, and all the people living on them, are spread out across Earth's surface. View the photos to learn more about some places on Earth.

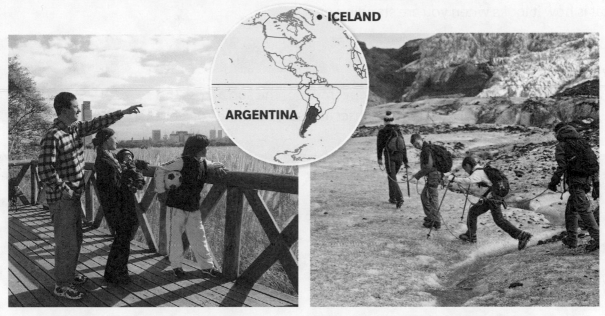

Here is a family in Argentina. Argentina lies south of the equator, in the Southern Hemisphere, or the southern half of Earth. It is on the continent of South America.

Here is a family hiking in Iceland. Iceland is an island north of the equator, between North America and Europe. It is in the Northern Hemisphere, or the northern half of Earth.

1. What do you think keeps all the people and other things on Earth's surface from falling off?

_____

_____

_____

_____

_____

 EVIDENCE NOTEBOOK Look for this icon to help you gather evidence to answer the question above.

Is Earth a Sphere?

Where Does the Sun Go?

Thousands of years ago people believed that Earth was flat because that is how it looks when you are standing on it.

Sun Moves

2. Study the picture. It shows the movement of the sun across the sky each day. Write the words *sunset* and *sunrise* in the correct box below.

Explore Online

At dawn, the sun appears to rise in the east.

In the afternoon, it seems to move across the sky.

At dusk, the sun appears to sink in the west.

3. If you lived at that time you would have noticed that the sun rises in the east, goes overhead during the day, and sets in the west at night. You might have wondered how the sun could have returned to the east by the next morning. How do you think people who believed in a flat Earth would have explained the sun's motion at night?

_____

_____

_____

_____

An Ant's View of the World

4. Try this activity. Start with a golf ball. Hold the ball 15 cm from your face. As you hold the ball, notice its shape. Keeping yourself and the ball still, look at what you can see above, below, and to the sides of the ball. Repeat these steps with the basketball and then the large beach ball. Draw what you see in the boxes below.

5. Look at the image of the beach ball. Now imagine you are a really tiny ant and you are climbing on a beach ball. As you looked out across the beach ball what would you see? Would you have any way of knowing that you are really on the surface of a huge ball?

_____

_____

_____

_____

6. How do these activities help you explain why Earth looks flat to us?

_____

_____

_____

_____

📘 **EVIDENCE NOTEBOOK** Gather evidence to explain why Earth appears flat to humans. Enter the evidence in your Evidence Notebook.

Flat or Round

We have all seen images of a round Earth from space. Are there ways to tell Earth is curved while standing on it? The images below show some evidence that can be used to prove Earth's shape.

The View from Above

7. Study the pictures, then answer the questions.

▷ Explore Online

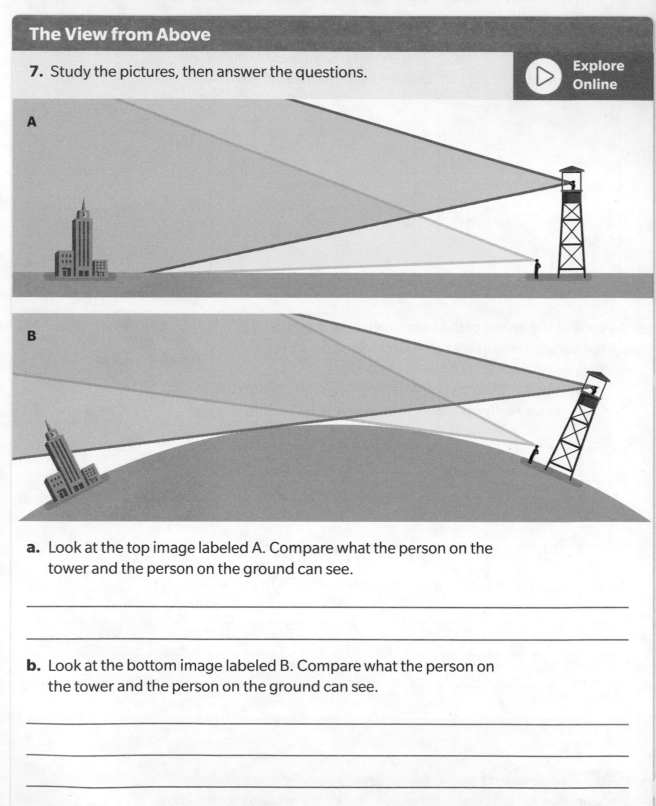

a. Look at the top image labeled A. Compare what the person on the tower and the person on the ground can see.

_____

_____

b. Look at the bottom image labeled B. Compare what the person on the tower and the person on the ground can see.

_____

_____

_____

One piece of evidence that Earth is round is that you can see more of Earth's surface when you climb up high. Is there more evidence?

The images below show what you would see if you watched a ship sail **over** the horizon, or area where the sea and sky appear to meet. Why does the entire ship appear as though it's rising from under the water?

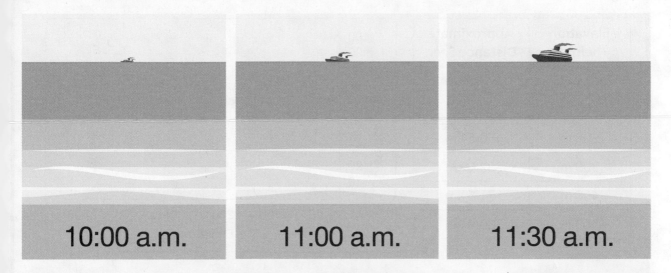

| 10:00 a.m. | 11:00 a.m. | 11:30 a.m. |

Which View Is Right?

8. The pictures below show two possible views of a ship sailing from the horizon toward a pier. Compare the views. Which view supports what you learned above about how a ship looks as it appears at the horizon? How does this provide evidence of Earth's round shape?

Explore Online

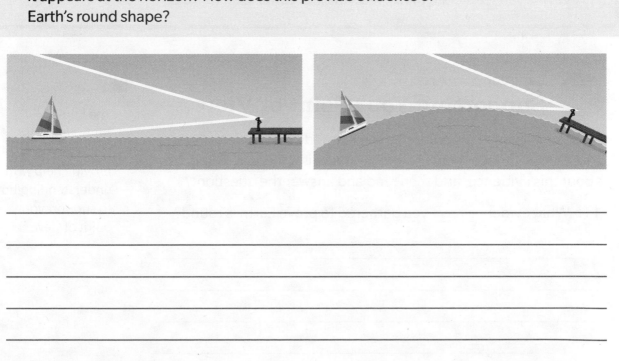

_____

_____

_____

_____

_____

_____

Do the Math
Above and Beyond

Elevation is the height above Earth's surface. The data in the table shows how much of Earth's surface you can see from different elevations.

Elevation (height)	Approximate Distance Seen
1 m	3.5 km
100 m	35.5 km
200 m	50.5 km
300 m	62.0 km
400 m	71.5 km
500 m	80.0 km

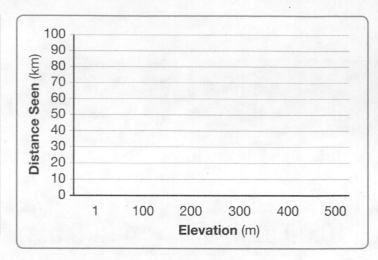

9. Use the data to make a bar graph above.

10. Select the best answer for the question. Why can you see more of Earth's surface the higher you are?

   a. You can see over the clouds.

   b. The air is cleaner so you can see farther.

   c. You can see around the curved surface of Earth.

Language SmArts
Supporting Your Point of View

Tip

The English Language Arts Handbook can provide help with understanding how to support your point of view.

Scientists used the evidence you learned so far to determine that Earth's surface is curved and its shape is spherical. Think about this evidence, and then read and answer the question.

11. What evidence have you gathered to prove Earth is round?

_____

_____

_____

_____

_____

_____

HANDS-ON ACTIVITY
A Trip around the World

Objective

Collaborate to learn how gravity affects objects on Earth's surface, using a model of Earth.

What question will you investigate to meet this objective?

_____

_____

_____

Procedure

STEP 1 Inflate the globe.

STEP 2 Tape at least one standing figure to each of the seven continents on the globe: North America, South America, Europe, Asia, Africa, Australia, and Antarctica.

STEP 3 Look through the globe, from North America through the center of Earth, and toward the figure you placed on Africa.

What direction are you looking when you look through Earth to see the figure standing in Africa?

    a. eastward

    b. northward

    c. downward

How would you describe the figure's position?

_____

_____

_____

279

STEP 4 Place your eyes near the feet of one of the figures. Look across the surface of the globe, as though you are that figure.

Can you see any of the other figures? What part of their body is closest to you?

_____

_____

_____

STEP 5 Holding the globe away from you with the North Pole on top and the South Pole on the bottom, look at the figure taped to Australia.

How would you describe the position of the figure on Australia?

_____

_____

_____

_____

Analyze Your Results

STEP 6 Still holding the globe away from you with the North Pole on top and the South Pole on the bottom, describe the figures that are attached to continents in the Southern Hemisphere—those on the southern half of the globe.

_____

_____

In real life, humans don't need to be taped to Earth to avoid falling off—no matter which continent they are on. Why not?

_____

_____

_____

STEP 7 Flip the globe so that the figure in Australia is upright. Look through the globe from the view of the Australian person. How does the person in North America look?

_____

_____

_____

Draw Conclusions

STEP 8 Which way does the force of gravity pull, and how was the tape used in this activity to mimic the force of gravity?

_____

_____

_____

STEP 9 How did the actual force of gravity make this activity difficult?

_____

_____

_____

STEP 10 Some of the figures in your model appeared sideways or upside down to you. However, people always feel upright no matter where they are standing on Earth's surface. State a claim explaining why this is true. Use evidence gathered from this activity to support your claim.

_____

_____

_____

_____

_____

_____

_____

What Is Gravity?

Staying Grounded

Why don't people, animals, water, and other objects on Earth float off into space? If Earth is round how is this possible?

When Things Fall Down

12. Look at the images shown here. The lumberjack is cutting down a tree. Draw what will happen to the tree.

13. How did you know what would happen when the tree was cut down?

_____

_____

_____

_____

14. What other example can you think of that would have the same cause-and-effect relationship?

_____

_____

_____

_____

What Do You Know about Gravity?

The tree was certainly affected by gravity. You probably already have some ideas about gravity. Let's see what you already know!

How Does It Drop?

15. Why did the tree fall to the ground? **Gravity** is a force that pulls all objects in the universe toward each other. How exactly does gravity work with objects on Earth?

Now it's time to practice what you've learned about gravity. Draw arrows to show which direction the pizza dough will drop if the man throws the dough into the air.

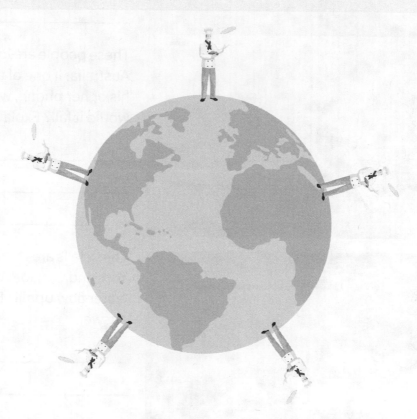

16. Explain why you drew the arrows the way you did. What do you already know about gravity that made you draw the arrows this way?

_____

_____

_____

_____

_____

Does Location Affect Gravity?

17. No matter what **hemisphere,** or half, of Earth you live on, gravity is pulling down on you. Use the photos to answer the questions.

▷ Explore Online

These penguins are located in Antarctica. Why don't they fall off Earth's surface? Explain your answer.

_____

_____

_____

These people are located in Australia. If one of them dropped his or her phone, which way would it fall? Explain your answer.

_____

_____

_____

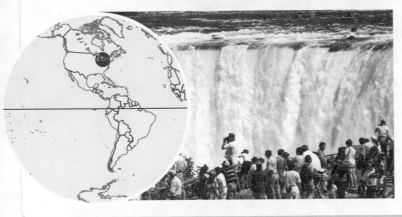

These falls are located in New York and Canada. Why doesn't water flow uphill? Explain your answer.

_____

_____

_____

18. How does gravity affect you?

_____

19. What is meant when someone says that an object "falls down"?

_____

_____

Tossing the Dough

We know that no matter where you are on Earth, all things fall down toward Earth's surface, but is that where gravity stops? Have you ever dug a hole and dropped something into it? If you have, you know that the object would continue to fall down. That is because gravity pulls all matter toward the center of our planet.

20. Look back at your drawing of the pizza dough. Use what you've learned about gravity to revise your drawing. In which direction will the pizza dough drop if the man throws the dough into the air?

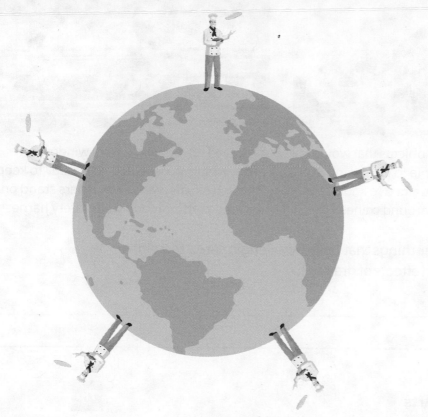

 EVIDENCE NOTEBOOK Explain in your Evidence Notebook how your idea of gravity has changed.

21. Choose the correct phrase to complete the sentence.

On Earth, gravity makes things fall _____.
   a. toward the center of Earth
   b. toward the equator
   c. toward the South Pole

Engineer It!
Gravity Challenges

Gravity is a force that affects all matter on Earth. People are in situations every day where the force of gravity makes falling a dangerous risk. It also makes lifting things harder. Look at each image to see how people have engineered ways to deal with the effects of gravity.

Cranes lift and move heavy objects that would be much too heavy for people to lift and move on their own. People must be trained to know how to operate and work safely around cranes.

Almost all tall buildings have windows. Those windows need to be cleaned. To keep themselves safe, window washers stand on elevated platforms and wear safety harnesses.

22. What are some other things that have been engineered to help people deal with the effects of gravity?

_____

_____

Language SmArts
Supporting a Point of View

You've learned that gravity pulls objects toward Earth's center. You've also learned that people have engineered things to deal with the effects of gravity.

23. How might you support the opinion that a rock climber's biggest problem is gravity?

_____

_____

_____

_____

Discover More

Check out this path . . . or go online to choose one of these other paths.

Engineer a Parachute

- **Weighing In**
- **Life in Space**

Skydivers use parachutes to float safely to the ground as gravity pulls them toward Earth's center. The parachutes are compressed into small packages when the skydivers jump out of the plane. Then the parachutes open during the skydivers' fall, allowing the skydivers to land safely. In this activity, use your design skills to engineer a parachute that allows a plastic "skydiver" to "jump" from at least 3 meters and float to the ground.

Find a Problem:

24. What is the problem you are trying to solve?

_____

_____

_____

_____

_____

_____

Brainstorm: Write down all the ideas you and your team come up with. Keep in mind the criteria and constraints.

Criteria and Constraints

- ☐ Your figure will drop from at least 3 meters, such as from a second story or playground equipment.
- ☐ Your parachute will float to the ground carrying a plastic figure.
- ☐ Your parachute will open.
- ☐ Your parachute will land no more than 2 meters from your targeted landing point.

Plan: Think about the material your parachute will be made of. Make some sketches of your design, and gather your materials together. Keep in mind the criteria and constraints.

25. What materials did you use to make your parachute?

_____

_____

_____

_____

Build: Build your parachute according to your design.

Test: Test your parachute by dropping the figure a few times from 3 meters or more. Make a data table to keep track of your results based on the criteria and constraints.

Evaluate and Redesign: Did you meet the criteria and constraints? Make any necessary changes to your design based on the test drops.

26. Was your parachute successful? Why or why not? What improvements to your design could you make?

_____

_____

_____

_____

Communicate: Compare your results with other teams.

Lesson Check

Name _____

Can You Explain It?

1. Now that you've learned about gravity, explain why people do not fall off Earth's surface. Be sure to do the following:

- Identify the force that keeps everything on Earth's surface.

- Explain why people on opposite sides of the globe do not feel upside down or sideways.

- Describe what it means for an object to fall down.

 EVIDENCE NOTEBOOK Use the information you've collected in your Evidence Notebook to help you answer these questions.

_____

_____

_____

_____

_____

_____

Checkpoints

2. Which of the following could you do to demonstrate to someone why Earth appears flat?

   a. Have the person hold a golf ball in front of his or her face and look across the top of the ball.

   b. Have the person hold a tennis ball in front of his or her face and look across the top of the ball.

   c. Have the person hold a large beach ball in front of his or her face and look across the top of the ball.

   d. Have the person hold a baseball in front of his or her face and look across the top of the ball.

3. Which of the following is evidence that Earth is a sphere? Choose all that apply.
  a. Higher elevations allow you to see around the curve of Earth's horizon.
  b. You see only the top part of a ship as it sails over the horizon.
  c. The sun and stars travel across the sky from east to west.

4. Choose the correct answer. You are standing on a beach watching a ship sailing across the ocean. What could you do to be able to watch the ship longer before it disappears across the horizon?
  a. Walk north across the beach.
  b. Wade out into the water.
  c. Climb to the top of a building.
  d. Lie down and look across the surface of the water.

5. Choose the correct phrase to complete the sentences.

| to the right | away from Earth's center |
| to the left | toward Earth's center |

The most accurate way to describe what a downward direction means is to say that "down" is the direction _____. The most accurate way to describe what an upward direction means is to say that "up" is the direction

_____.

6. Which of the following are true about gravity? Select all that apply.
  a. Gravity is a force.
  b. Gravity affects all matter on Earth.
  c. There is no gravity in the Southern Hemisphere.
  d. Gravity is caused by air pushing down on things.

Lesson Roundup

A. Choose the correct words to complete each sentence.

Evidence showing that Earth has a _____ shape includes the

ability to see farther when you climb _____.

round
flat
up high
down low

B. Which image correctly shows a model of Earth and the direction of the force of gravity?

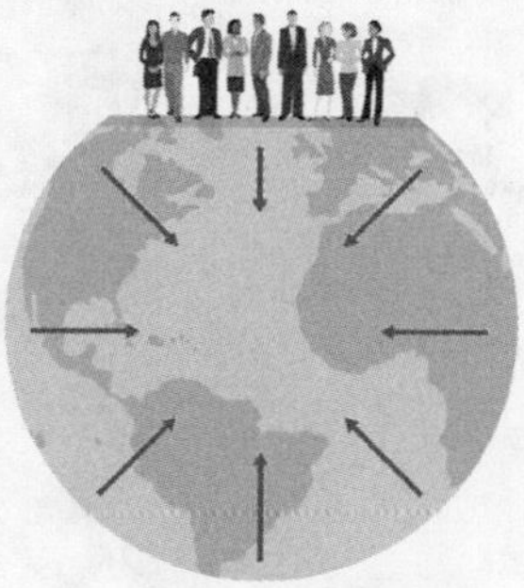

1.

2.

3.

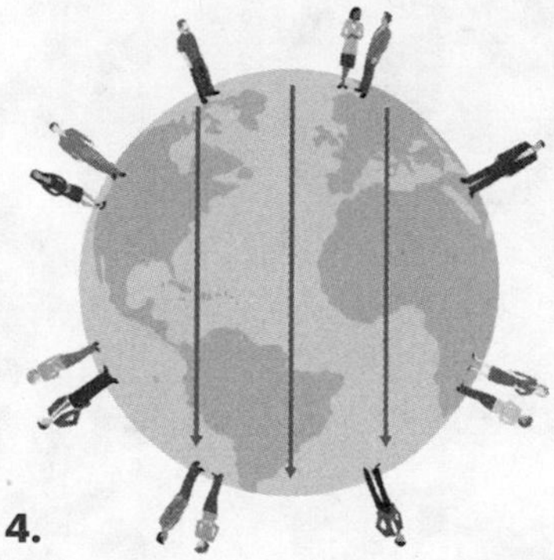

4.

C. Explain your answer choice for the question above.

_____

_____

_____

_____

D. Keep track of anything else you learned about gravity by writing it here.

_____

_____

_____

What Daily Patterns Can Be Observed?

We've all seen beautiful sunsets. What causes this? Is the sun really setting or is the Earth turning?

By the end of this lesson . . .
you'll be able to describe patterns caused by interactions between Earth, the sun, and the stars.

Can You Explain It?

 Explore Online

A sundial is an invention that takes advantage of the predictable ways that sunlight and features of Earth's surface interact, or work together, to cast shadows.

1. Why is the shadow of the sundial changing?

_____

_____

_____

_____

_____

_____

_____

_____

_____

_____

_____

_____

_____

 EVIDENCE NOTEBOOK Look for this icon to help you gather evidence to answer the question above.

What Is on the Move?

Patterns in the Sky

Shadows aren't the only things that change over the course of a day. A lot happens in the sky from one sunrise to the next. Look at the images below to see changes in the sky for one day.

After you have compared the images of the sky, answer the questions below.

2. What did you notice about the sun over the course of the day?

_____

_____

_____

3. What did you notice about the moon and stars over the course of the night?

_____

_____

_____

The Moving Sun

Each day, the sun appears to rise in the east, move across the sky, then set in the west. In the mornings and late afternoons, the sun is low in the sky. Around noon, the sun is high in the sky.

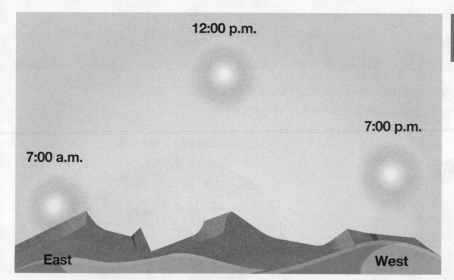

The sun's position is often observed by measuring the angle of the sun above the surface of Earth.

Study the table below. It shows the sun's altitude for two days in late May, as seen from a city in the United States.

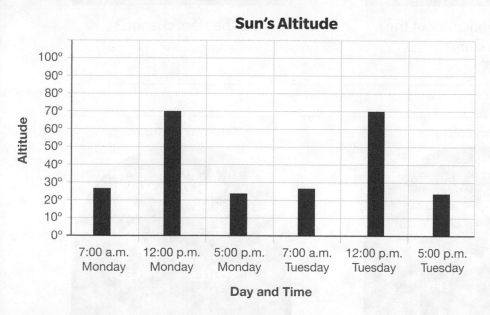

4. Study the graph. What patterns do you see?

_____

_____

5. Based on the graph, predict when the sun will be the lowest in the sky 2 weeks later.

   a. 8:15 a.m.   **b.** 12:30 p.m.   **c.** 1:45 p.m.

The Night Sky

On a clear night, you can see many **constellations,** or groups of stars that make patterns in the night sky. Like the sun, stars appear to move across the sky from east to west. Let's camp out over night to see if the positions of constellations change within one night.

Under the Stars

6. These images show how the night sky changed overnight from Friday to Saturday. Answer the questions under the images.

Friday 10:00 p.m.

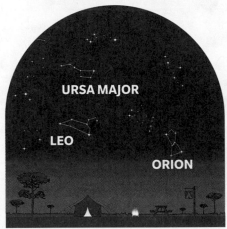

Saturday 12:00 a.m.

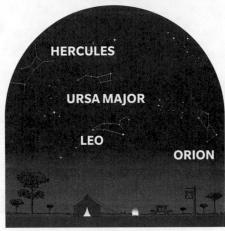

a. What do you notice about the position of the stars?

_____

_____

b. How did the stars change?

_____

_____

Saturday 2:00 a.m.

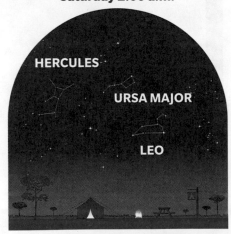

Saturday 4:00 a.m.

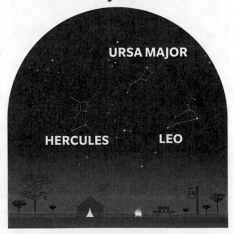

c. What patterns do you see?

_____

_____

d. How has Orion changed this night?

_____

_____

Rotating Earth or Rotating Sun and Stars?

Long ago, people had different ideas about what caused the sun and stars to appear to move. One idea was that the sun and stars moved while Earth remained still. Another idea was that Earth rotates on its **axis,** or the imaginary line that runs through Earth from pole to pole. This spinning of Earth on its axis is called **rotation.** Do the following activities to try to discover which model is correct.

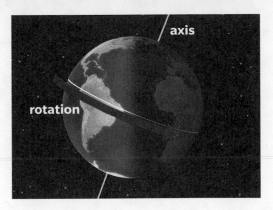

Part 1

STEP 1a: Your teacher will have placed images of the sun and constellations on the walls in the room. Imagine that your head is planet Earth. Stand, facing the sun, and hold your hands on either side of your face so that they make "horizons" that you can see on the left and right. This position represents the sun, Earth, and stars at 12:00 p.m.

STEP 1b: Slowly rotate to the right and watch things appear to "rise" above one hand, move across your vision, and "set" behind the other hand. Stop every 3 seconds and record the location of the sun and stars and predict what time is represented. Continue to move and record observations for five minutes.

Part 2

STEP 2a: For this model, students will hold the images of the sun and stars along the edges of the classroom. You will continue to represent Earth using your hands to make the horizons. Begin again by facing the sun at 12:00 p.m. This time Earth will stay still, but the sun and stars will move around Earth to make day and night.

STEP 2b: The sun and constellations should move slowly around Earth, stopping every 3 seconds. Earth says still. Each time they stop, Earth should record the location of the sun and stars and predict what time it is. Continue to move and record observations for five minutes. Note the location of the sun and stars.

7. Based on the activities, which model seemed correct? Provide evidence.

_____

_____

_____

Your Turn

8. Draw a diagram to model and explain your understanding of why the sun and stars change over the course of 24 hours. Include Earth, the sun, and stars in your diagram.

EVIDENCE NOTEBOOK How can the patterns you've just observed help explain why the shadow of the sundial changed? Enter your ideas in your Evidence Notebook.

Language SmArts
Cause and Effect

9. Explain some of the patterns you observed, and explain what causes those patterns.

_____

_____

_____

_____

_____

_____

_____

Tip

The English Language Arts Handbook can provide help with understanding how to find cause and effect.

What Causes Day and Night?

As the World Turns

Read the following conversation between a student and her friends to discover an effect of Earth's rotation. Gabriella lives in the United States and has just finished school. She decided to call some of her friends who live all over the world.

Explore Online

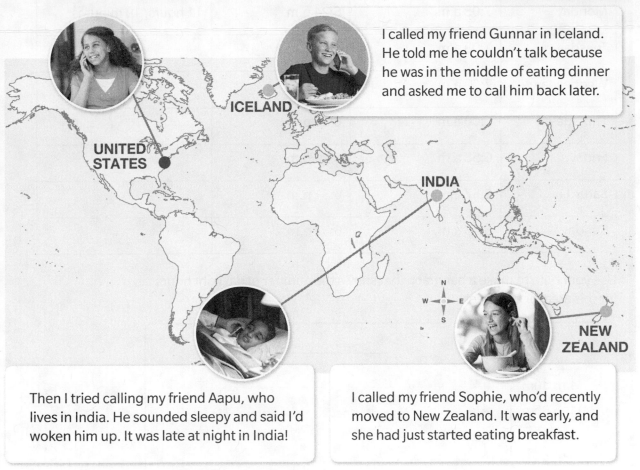

I called my friend Gunnar in Iceland. He told me he couldn't talk because he was in the middle of eating dinner and asked me to call him back later.

Then I tried calling my friend Aapu, who lives in India. He sounded sleepy and said I'd woken him up. It was late at night in India!

I called my friend Sophie, who'd recently moved to New Zealand. It was early, and she had just started eating breakfast.

10. Compare the time of day in each place that Sophie called.

_____

_____

11. Why do you think the time of day is different in each place?

_____

_____

_____

12. Look at the chart. It shows times of sunrise and sunset for an area over the course of one week. Calculate the number of daylight hours for each day. Then look for patterns. The first calculation has been done for you.

Hours of Daylight			
Day	Time of sunrise	Time of sunset	Daylight hours
Monday	7:05 a.m.	6:24 p.m.	11 hours, 19 minutes
Tuesday	7:03 a.m.	6:25 p.m.	
Wednesday	7:02 a.m.	6:27 p.m.	
Thursday	7:00 a.m.	6:28 p.m.	
Friday	6:58 a.m.	6:29 p.m.	
Saturday	6.57 a.m.	6:31 p.m.	
Sunday	6:55 a.m.	6:32 p.m.	

Use your data to make a bar graph that shows the number of daylight hours for this area for one week.

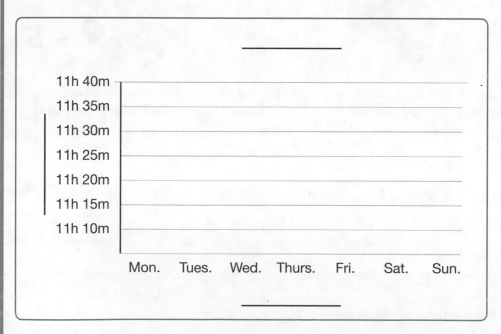

13. If this pattern continues, I predict that there will be _____ of

sunlight on the following Wednesday.

History of Telling Time

Did you know that ancient people kept track of time using shadows cast by the sun? View the images to see how technology engineered to tell time has improved throughout history.

A **sundial** may be the most ancient means of telling time. The shadow of the stick is long in the morning, shortest at noon, and becomes longer as sunset approaches. More accurate sundials have the hours marked on the disk.

An **hourglass** has two bulbs connected by a narrow neck. Grains of sand trickle down from the top to the bottom. This movement can be used to keep track of time. When all the grains have moved to the bottom, an hour has passed.

Mechanical clocks were invented in the late 1300s. They used springs or weights to mark each hour with the sound of a bell. Later clocks had hour hands and minute hands to make it easier to tell time.

The first **atomic clock** was invented in 1949. These clocks are extremely accurate. They are so accurate that it would take 300 million years before the time would be incorrect by one second.

Choose the correct answer.

14. What disadvantage does a sundial have?

    a. It cannot work during the night.

    b. It cannot be used to track the hours of the day.

    c. It uses costly materials and is difficult to build.

Around We Go

Look at the two images. The person represents your position in space at the given time. As Earth rotates, your view changes.

 Explore Online

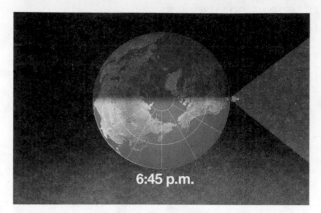

6:45 p.m.

3:00 a.m.

15. Choose the correct words to complete each sentence.

Earth's _____ causes the _____ to appear to rise in the east in the morning, move across the sky, and set in the west in the late afternoon. Earth's movement also causes the stars to appear to _____ from the east to the west each night. In addition, this movement of the sun causes _____ and night.

rotation
be still
move
day
moon
shape
sun

 EVIDENCE NOTEBOOK Do you think you can see shadows at night? Why or why not? Record your ideas in your Evidence Notebook.

 Language SmArts
Summarize

Use a flashlight and a globe to represent the sun and Earth. Start with the sun shining on Africa. This will represent 12:00 p.m., when the sun is highest in the sky. Then, model the movement of Earth over 24 hours showing the sunset, nighttime, and sunrise for Africa.

16. Write a paragraph to summarize how day and night occur.

_____

_____

_____

_____

_____

Tip

The English Language Arts Handbook can provide help with understanding how to summarize.

How Does A Shadow Grow?

Objective

Collaborate to model how shadows change throughout the day.

What question will you investigate to meet this objective?

_____

_____

Materials
- new, unsharpened pencil
- modeling clay
- poster board
- metric ruler
- marker
- rocks (4)

Procedure

STEP 1 Use the clay to position the pencil upright in the center of the poster board.

Why is it important to position the pencil correctly?

_____

_____

_____

_____

_____

STEP 2 Place the poster board outside in a sunny, flat area away from trees and other tall objects. Put a rock on each corner of the poster board.

What might happen if you did not weigh down the poster board?

_____

_____

_____

STEP 3 Measure the length of the pencil's shadow. Mark the end of the shadow. Record the time of day and your measurement on the poster board.

Why should you write down the time of day and your measurement?

_____

_____

_____

STEP 4 Observe the position of the sun and the direction of the shadow in relation to the sun. Record your observations in the table below, along with your measurements of the shadow. **Caution:** Do not look directly at the sun.

Why is it important to observe the position of the sun?

_____

_____

STEP 5 Repeat steps 3 and 4 each hour throughout the school day.

Why should you take measurements throughout the day?

_____

_____

Complete the data table as you observe and measure.

Shadow Data Table			
Time of day	Position of sun	Length of shadow	Direction of shadow in relation to sun

Analyze Your Results

STEP 6 Use your data to create a line graph. Label the horizontal axis (*x*-axis) *Time of day.* Label the vertical axis (*y*-axis) *Length of shadow.*

STEP 7 Analyze your graph. What pattern do you observe?

_____

_____

_____

_____

STEP 8 Compare your results with your classmates. Why is it important for scientists to share the results of their investigations?

_____

_____

Draw Conclusions

STEP 9 Make a claim about the sun's movement based on the question you investigated. Cite evidence from your investigation to support this claim.

_____

_____

STEP 10 If you could observe the shadow of a stick from morning to evening on a sunny day, what do you think you would observe?

_____

_____

305

Discover More

Check out this path . . . or go online to choose one of these other paths.

Careers in Science & Engineering

- **Foucault Pendulum**
- **Time Flies**

Astronomer

Astronomers are scientists who study space. They study objects ranging from small, rocky asteroids to enormous galaxies that contain planets and billions of stars. Astronomers have a strong background in physics, which focuses on matter, forces, and energy.

Physics helps astronomers understand the structure of the universe. Astronomers also study chemistry, computer science, and math. After completing their college studies, many astronomers obtain a doctorate in their field. This can take up to seven more years of college.

On average, astronomers spend only 10 to 30 nights a year viewing the night sky. They may travel to remote observatories, or buildings that house large telescopes. These buildings are far from city lights, so views of the night sky are clearer. Astronomers often spend the remainder of the work year analyzing, or examining, the data they gathered.

Astronomers often specialize in one field of study, such as how stars change over time or why some galaxies have spiral shapes. They may work in teams, using computers to analyze the data they have gathered. Often, they create computer models to predict or understand data.

More than half of astronomers work with colleges and universities. They teach students about the universe, as well as conduct research.

About a third of astronomers work for the government in some manner. NASA, for example, employs astronomers to analyze data and help develop space missions.

17. Training in which field best helps astronomers understand the structure of the universe?

   a. biology

   b. physics

   c. geology

   d. ecology

18. Which statement about astronomers is true?

   a. They spend less time looking through telescopes than they spend analyzing data.

   b. They rarely interact with students.

   c. They work mainly in government jobs.

   d. Research takes up a small amount of their time.

19. Which statement best explains why astronomers need a background in computer science?

   a. They view images of space objects on computers.

   b. They communicate with one another using computers.

   c. They design computer models about space.

What Is NASA?

Many astronomers and engineers would love to work for NASA. What is NASA? Do some research and answer the questions below.

20. What does NASA stand for?

_____

_____

_____

_____

_____

21. What does NASA do?

_____

_____

_____

_____

_____

22. Where is NASA located?

_____

_____

_____

23. Describe one opportunity NASA provides for kids.

_____

_____

_____

24. Describe something interesting you found while researching about NASA.

_____

_____

Lesson Check

Name _____

Explore Online

Can You Explain It?

1. Now that you've learned about Earth's rotation and the apparent, or supposed, movement of the sun, explain why the shadow on the sundial changes throughout the day. Write your answer below. Be sure to do the following:

- Relate Earth's rotation to the apparent movement of the sun.

- Describe how the angle of the sun changes throughout the day.

- Explain how the changing angle of the sun affects shadows.

EVIDENCE NOTEBOOK Use the information you've collected in your Evidence Notebook to help you cover each point above.

_____

_____

_____

_____

_____

_____

Checkpoints

2. Which statements about the diagram are true? Circle all that apply.

   a. The stars will appear in the same position in two hours.

   b. The stars will appear to change position over the course of the night.

   c. The stars appear to move because of Earth's rotation.

   d. The stars appear motionless because of the sun's rotation.

3. Choose the correct words to complete the sentences.

| east   west   high   low |

Each day, the sun appears to rise in the _____, move across the sky, then set in the _____. In the mornings and late afternoons, the sun is _____ in the sky. Around noon, the sun is _____ in the sky.

4. Last week, a student measured the length of a shadow at three different times during the day. She forgot to record her measurements in her data chart. Fill in the chart with the correct measurement.

| 2.1 meters   0.2 meters   4.0 meters |

Time	8:00 a.m.	10:00 a.m.	12:00 p.m.
Shadow length			

5. The diagram shows a position on Earth at 3:00 a.m. What is likely to happen to that position in five hours?
   a. It will remain stationary.
   b. It will rotate and face the sun.
   c. It will rotate and face away from the sun.

3:00 a.m.

6. You learned that Earth's rotation is responsible for many changes we see in the sky each day. Which of the following movements seen is not caused by Earth's rotation?
   a. sun
   b. birds
   c. stars
   d. shadows

Lesson Roundup

A. The drawings show the sun at different times of day. Write which time it is in each picture: 1:00 p.m., 7:00 p.m., or 6:00 a.m.

_____   _____   _____

B. Explain how the stars' movements are similar to the sun's movement.

_____

_____

C. The table shows times of sunrise and sunset for several days in May. Study the table, and then answer the questions below.

Day	Sunrise	Sunset
Monday	6:39 a.m.	8:29 p.m.
Tuesday	6:38 a.m.	8:30 p.m.
Wednesday	6:37 a.m.	8:31 p.m.
Thursday	6:36 a.m.	8:32 p.m.

Predict times of sunrise and sunset on Friday.

1. sunrise: 6:40 a.m.; sunset: 8:28 p.m.

2. sunrise: 6:35 a.m.; sunset: 8:30 p.m.

3. sunrise: 6:35 a.m.; sunset: 8:33 p.m.

4. sunrise: 6:39 a.m.; sunset: 8:35 p.m.

What pattern do you see in the data?

_____

_____

D. Keep track of anything else you learned about here!

_____

_____

What Patterns Can Be Observed in a Year?

From this vantage point, you can see the moon, sun, stars, and Earth. From Earth's surface, there are patterns to how the sun, moon, and stars appear in the sky.

By the end of this lesson . . .
you'll be able to describe monthly and seasonal patterns of the sun, moon, and stars.

Can You Explain It?

January 9:00 p.m.   July 9:00 p.m.

Max walks his dog at 9:00 p.m. each night of the year. He looks up at the night sky and tries to identify the constellations—groups of stars that form patterns in the sky. The image on the left shows Max's view of the night sky in January at 9:00 p.m. The image on the right shows his view of the night sky in July at 9:00 p.m.

1. Explain why the constellations he sees in the night sky changed. Keep in mind that he is viewing the sky at the same time each night.

_____

_____

_____

_____

_____

_____

_____

_____

Tip

Learn more about patterns and the stars in What Daily Patterns Can Be Observed?

 EVIDENCE NOTEBOOK Look for this icon to help you gather evidence to answer the question above.

What Patterns Do the Sun and Moon Cause During the Year?

Round and Round

Each year, Earth makes one complete orbit around the sun. Earth is not the only object orbiting in space. All the planets orbit the sun, and all the moons orbit their planets.

Explore Online

The moon is a natural satellite of Earth. It takes the moon about a month to make one orbit around Earth. An **orbit** is the path of one object in space around another.

Earth orbits the sun in an almost perfect circle. This movement of Earth one time around the sun is called a **revolution.** It takes about 365 days for Earth to make one orbit around the sun. Our year is based on this movement of Earth.

2. What patterns do you think are caused by the orbits of Earth and the moon?

_____

_____

_____

_____

_____

 EVIDENCE NOTEBOOK How do you think the Earth-sun-moon system affects our view of the stars at different times of the year? Write your ideas in your Evidence Notebook.

Moon Shapes

Have you ever seen a full moon on a clear night? How about a crescent moon early in the morning? Each month, the moon goes through phases, or changes in its appearance as seen from Earth. Look at the images below to see how the moon appears to change shape.

Explore Online

3. The calendar above shows moon phases for July and August. Study the moon phases. Look for a pattern. Then fill in the missing moon phases in the September calendar by drawing moons of the correct shape.

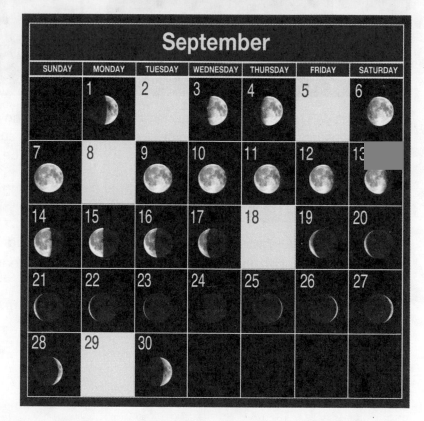

4. About how many days does it take the moon to go from one full moon to the next full moon?

   a. 10   **b.** 20   **c.** 30   **d.** 40

5. Describe the patterns you observed in the calendars.

_____

_____

_____

Sun Seasons

The moon's orbit causes moon phases. What patterns are caused by Earth's revolution around the sun? View the images below to see one effect of Earth's revolution on the day sky in the Northern Hemisphere.

Look at the sun's position in the sky during different seasons, as seen from the same spot. Note the time and month.

This also shows the sun's position in the midday sky during summer, fall, winter, and spring. Note these are the same months, but a different year.

Chart the Sun

6. The graph below lists the typical positions of the midday sun in different seasons. Using the data from above, complete the graph for Year 1 and Year 2.

Sun's Position at 12:00 p.m.

	High
Position	Medium
	Low

January Year 1   April Year 1   July Year 1   October Year 1   January Year 2   April Year 2   July Year 2   October Year 2

Dates

7. During which season does the sun appear highest in the sky at noon?

    a. winter   **c.** summer

    b. spring   **d.** fall

8. During which season does the sun appear lowest in the sky at noon?

    a. winter   **c.** summer

    b. spring   **d.** fall

9. Describe the pattern of the sun's height in the sky from season to season.

_____

_____

_____

_____

10. Use the patterns you learned to draw the midday suns below to show their position in the sky each season.

| 12:00 p.m. January Year 3 | 12:00 p.m. April Year 3 | 12:00 p.m. July Year 3 | 12:00 p.m. October Year 3 |

317

Moon Myths

11. The moon appears as the largest object in the night sky and is our closest neighbor in space. Ancient people were fascinated by the moon, just as we are today. They made up myths, or traditional stories that help explain natural events, about the phases of the moon. Research online to learn about different moon myths.

Write your own myth about the moon. Use posters, diagrams, videos, or other visuals to illustrate your myth. You might also want to include sound effects. Share your myth with the class. Use the lines below to take notes.

_____

_____

_____

_____

_____

_____

Language SmArts

Compare and Contrast

12. Think about all you have learned so far. Earth's revolution around the sun and the moon's orbit around Earth cause patterns in the sky. Compare and contrast Earth's orbit and the moon's orbit. What patterns do they affect?

_____

_____

_____

_____

_____

Tip

The English Language Arts Handbook can provide help with understanding how to compare and contrast.

Sunrise, Sunset

Objective

Collaborate to learn how the motions of Earth in space affect seasonal patterns of sunrise and sunset. These motions also affect the amount of daylight each day has in a given location on Earth.

> **Materials**
> - globe
> - Internet access
> - graph paper

What question will you investigate to meet this objective?

_____

_____

_____

Procedure

STEP 1 Find your location on a globe.

About how far from the equator is your location?

_____

_____

_____

_____

STEP 2 Predict how times of sunrise and sunset might change for each season at your location. Also make a prediction about the amount of daylight for each season.

What reasoning did you use to make your predictions?

_____

_____

_____

_____

319

STEP 3 Research times of sunrise and sunset for your area for each season. Then calculate the amount of daylight hours for each season, using these four dates: January 15, April 15, July 15, and October 15. Gather data for a three-year period. Record your data in the chart.

Why do you think it's important to gather data for a three-year period? And why use those specific dates?

_____

_____

_____

_____

Date	Sunrise	Sunset	Hours of daylight
Jan 15, 20___ ___			
April 15, 20___ ___			
July 15, 20___ ___			
Oct. 15, 20___ ___			
Jan 15, 20___ ___			
April 15, 20___ ___			
July 15, 20___ ___			
Oct. 15, 20___ ___			
Jan 15, 20___ ___			
April 15, 20___ ___			
July 15, 20___ ___			
Oct. 15, 20___ ___			

Analyze Your Results

STEP 4 On a sheet of graph paper, draw a bar graph of hours of daylight for all 12 seasons of data you collected.

STEP 5 What kind of pattern do you see in your graph?

_____

_____

_____

STEP 6 Look back at your data table. How do times of sunrise and sunset change each season?

_____

_____

_____

STEP 7 Compare your results with your classmates. How does sharing results help scientists draw strong conclusions?

_____

_____

_____

Draw Conclusions

STEP 8 You have learned that the sun is lower in the sky in winter and higher in summer. Do you think this affects the hours of daylight in summer versus winter? Explain your answer.

_____

_____

_____

STEP 9 Make a claim based on your investigation. Cite evidence from your investigation to support this claim.

_____

_____

_____

Different Stars, Different Seasons

Campus Tour

What you see around you often depends on certain things. Look at the images below and think about why there are limitations to what the boy sees. Then discuss your ideas with a classmate.

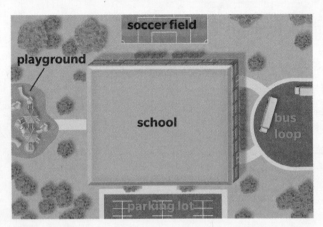

From above, the view of the school grounds is clear and unobstructed. On the ground, it's harder to see the whole picture.

DeShawn is playing soccer in the back of the school. He is unable to see the parking lot. Why not? Does it still exist? Use the map to help you.

Where is DeShawn in this image? Why can't he see the playground? Use the map to help you.

DeShawn can't see the flag pole from his position. Why can't he see it?

13. Why couldn't DeShawn view certain things as he walked around campus?

_____

_____

_____

The Night Moves

14. Your teacher will have placed a model of the sun in the middle of the room and posted names of constellations around the room. Imagine that your head is planet Earth, and that it is daytime when you face toward the sun, and nighttime when you turn and observe the constellations of stars. Follow these steps.

STEP 1 Stand in front of the model sun with your back facing the sun. You are modeling Earth during a summer night. Record your observations of the constellations you see in front of you.

STEP 2 Revolve one-quarter of the way around the sun in a counterclockwise direction. Keep the sun at your back. This position represents Earth during a fall night. Record your observations of the constellations.

STEP 3 Revolve another quarter of the way around the sun in a counterclockwise direction. Keep the sun at your back. This position represents Earth during a winter night. Record your observations of the constellations.

STEP 4 Revolve another quarter of the way around the sun in a counterclockwise direction. Keep the sun at your back. This position represents Earth during a spring night. Record your observations of the constellations.

How did this activity help you to understand why different stars are visible during different times of the year?

_____

_____

_____

_____

_____

_____

Shifting Stars

Earth's revolution affects how we view the sun's position in the sky. How does Earth's orbit affect our view of the stars at night? Go through images below to see Earth make a complete orbit around the sun, and view the constellations that are visible from Earth as it moves. Discuss the questions below with a classmate.

10:00 p.m.

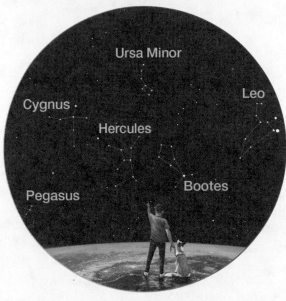

On a **summer** night, you see these constellations in the night sky from a given spot on Earth. Which constellations can you see?

10:00 p.m.

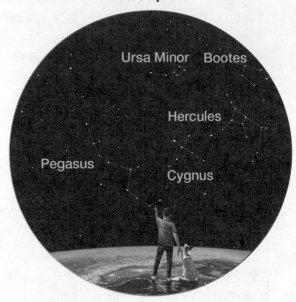

On a **fall** night, you see these constellations in the night sky from the same spot on Earth. How has Hercules changed from the summer view?

10:00 p.m.

On a **winter** night, you see these constellations in the night sky from the same spot on Earth. Again, the night sky features some different constellations. How has Ursa Minor changed?

10:00 p.m.

On a **spring** night, you see these constellations in the night sky from the same spot on Earth. Once again, the night sky looks different. Can you see Pegasus? What do you think happened?

Spring

Cygnus

Pegasus

Orion

Ursa Minor

Hercules

Gemini

Leo

Bootes

15. Look back at the spring image on the prior page and take note of the constellations in the sky. Then, look at the star map here which shows where Earth is located in the spring. Circle the following: Earth and Pegasus. Explain why you can't see Pegasus in the spring.

_____

_____

_____

Changing Constellations

16. How did your observations of the constellations change with the seasons? Using the night images, complete the chart to record your observations. Write a large X if you saw the constellations during each season. Leave a space blank if you did not see the constellation in that season.

	Summer	Fall	Winter	Spring
Orion				
Gemini				
Leo				
Ursa Minor				
Pegasus				
Hercules				
Bootes				
Cygnus				

17. Which pair of constellations is visible in winter?

  a. Orion and Leo

  b. Gemini and Hercules

  c. Ursa Minor and Bootes

  d. Cygnus and Pegasus

Campus Constellations

Earlier in the lesson, you analyzed how a student's ability to see different parts of his school's campus was affected by his position. He was not able to see certain things depending on his location and direction. You can use that activity to help you understand why we see different stars in different seasons.

18. Complete the paragraph below by choosing the correct words from the list.

Earth	stars	moon	sun	planets

DeShawn moved around the building like _____ move(s) around the sun. The school building is like the _____: it is at the center of a system, and it affects how someone can see things on the other side of the system. The bus, playground, and basketball court were like _____. The boy could not see them all at the same time.

EVIDENCE NOTEBOOK What causes different constellations to be visible during different seasons? Enter your ideas in your Evidence Notebook.

Language SmArts
Summarize

19. Earlier in the lesson, you modeled Earth's revolution around the sun and saw how your view of the constellations changed as Earth moved. You also observed the constellations for each season. How would you summarize your observations?

_____

_____

_____

_____

_____

_____

_____

Tip

The English Language Arts Handbook can provide help with understanding how to summarize.

Discover More

Check out this path . . . or go online to choose one of the other paths.

Leap Year

• Constellations
• Seasonal Shadows

Leap Year

The following conversation took place between two friends in the summer of 2014:

Maria: Lisa, when were you born?

Lisa: I was born on February 29, 2004. So I'm ten years old.

Maria: But February 29 only happens during a leap year. There's only been two leap years since you were born. Are you sure you are ten?

Help Lisa find evidence to support her claim that she is ten years old. Study a calendar, and do some research to find out what a leap year is.

February

29

20. What is a leap year?

_____

_____

_____

_____

21. Why would Lisa's friend think that being born on February 29 of a leap year means Lisa is only two years old?

_____

_____

_____

_____

327

22. Like most patterns, there are exceptions to them. Research to find out why leap year doesn't always happen every four years.

_____

_____

_____

23. Use your research to complete the chart. The first two rows are completed for you.

	Year	Lisa's age
February 29th	2004	0
February 29th	2008	4
February 29th		
February 29th		
February 29th		
February 29th		

24. What pattern do you see in the chart?

_____

_____

_____

25. What evidence shows that Lisa is ten years old as of the summer of 2014?

_____

_____

_____

_____

26. When Lisa turns 64, what year will it be? Show your work in the space below.

_____

Lesson Check

Name _____

Can You Explain It?

1. Now that you've learned about Earth's revolution, explain why the constellations in the night sky change with the seasons. Write your answer on the lines below. Be sure to do the following:

• Explain Earth's revolution.

• Relate Earth's revolution to your view of the constellations throughout the year.

 EVIDENCE NOTEBOOK Use the information you've collected in your Evidence Notebook to help you cover each point above.

_____

_____

_____

_____

_____

_____

Checkpoints

2. The calendar indicates major phases of the moon for April. When will the next full moon occur after this month?

   a. May 20

   b. May 5

   c. May 31

   d. June 3

APRIL						
Monday	Tuesday	Wednesday	Thursday	Friday	Saturday	Sunday
				1	2	3
4	5	6	7 New moon	8	9	10
11	12	13	14 First quarter	15	16	17
18	19	20	21	22 Full moon	23	24
25	26	27	28	29 Last quarter	30	

3. The images show views of the night sky at a given location in summer (top) and winter (bottom). Which of the following statements is the most accurate explanation of why the night sky changes?

   a. Because Earth revolves around the sun, Earth is in different positions each season. In summer, Earth is on one side of the sun, and then in winter, it is on the opposite side. This changes what can be seen.

   b. Because Earth revolves around the sun, on some nights the sky is in one direction in the universe, and the next night it's in the other direction. It's just random that these two images happen to be different.

   c. The rotation, or spin, of Earth means the sky always looks different from month to month. It is hard to predict which constellations can be seen each season.

4. Which time unit is based on Earth's revolution around the sun?

   a. day   b. month   c. year   d. week

5. Choose the correct words to complete the sentences.

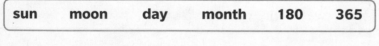

| sun | moon | day | month | 180 | 365 |

Earth revolves around the _____ in a circular path. It takes

about _____ days for Earth to make one revolution around

the sun. The _____ is a natural satellite of Earth. It takes

approximately a _____ to complete one orbit around Earth.

6. Your class is planning a trip to the science center. You will arrive at the science center at 10:00 a.m. and leave at 6:30 p.m. For your class to view stars with their telescope, it needs to be dark outside. What is the best time of year to plan the trip?

   a. fall   b. winter   c. spring   d. summer

Lesson Roundup

A. Look at the moon calendar. What pattern do you observe?

  a. The moon takes about one month to go through its phases.

  b. The moon looks the same for a week, and then changes.

  c. The moon appears to change shape once per month.

B. Look at images of the midday sun's position in different seasons. What pattern do you observe?

  a. The midday sun is lower in the sky in summer than in spring.

  b. The midday sun is higher in the sky in winter than in fall.

  c. The midday sun is lower in the sky during each season.

  d. The midday sun is in a similar position in spring and fall.

C. A friend hears the weather forecast for tomorrow night is very clear and cool. Excited, your friend suggests that you go camping on a nearby mountaintop so you can look at a constellation she admired in the sky five months earlier. Explain to your friend why she won't be able to see the same stars she saw five months ago.

_____

_____

_____

_____

What Is the Sun?

This might look like hot lava, but it's actually a close-up of the sun. What does this picture show us about the sun?

_____

By the end of this lesson . . .
you'll be able to describe why the sun appears so large and bright.

Can You Explain It?

Each day, the sun rises in the sky—it never takes a day off. You know what the sun looks like from Earth. But what would the sun look like from Saturn?

1. Why does the sun look so different from Saturn than it does from Earth?

_____

_____

_____

_____

_____

_____

Tip

To learn more about how the sun's energy benefits life, read _How Does Energy Get Transformed by Plants?_

 EVIDENCE NOTEBOOK Look for this icon to help you gather evidence to answer the question above.

333

What Are the Sun's Characteristics?

A Close-Up View

On a sunny day, you can feel the sun warming you and your surroundings. You can see its light shining all around you. Without the sun, life would not be possible on Earth.

2. What else do you know about the sun?

_____

_____

_____

This image shows the sun from far away. From Earth, we are used to seeing the sun from a long distance away.

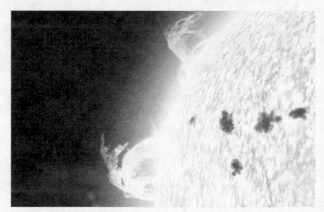

This image shows a close-up view of the sun. Because the sun is very far away, we have never actually been this close.

Think about the different images of the sun. How does the sun look from far away? What color is it? How big is it? How bright is it? Fill in the top row of the chart. Then look at the other image to compare how the sun looks from close up. Compare this close-up view to the Earth view. Enter your observations in the bottom row of the chart.

View	Color	Size and brightness	Characteristics
Far away			
Close-up			

Supporting Details

The sun is big, but exactly how big is it? Why is it bright? Let's find out more about the sun. Read the two paragraphs, and then answer the questions.

Solar System Giant

The sun is the largest object in our solar system. It makes up nearly 99.9 percent of the mass of our solar system. The sun has a diameter of about 1.4 million km (about 869,920 mi). You could line up about 110 Earths across the width of the sun and fit more than one million Earths inside it! The sun makes its own energy. The sun's light provides most of the energy for Earth.

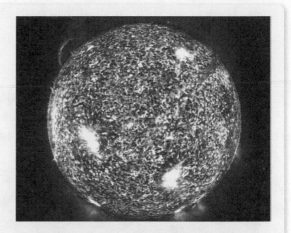

Traveling by Light Speed

The sun is at the center of our solar system. All the planets in our solar system revolve around the sun. The sun is about 150 million km from Earth, but it only takes about eight minutes for light from the sun to reach Earth. Other planets of the solar system are much closer or much farther away. Mercury is the closest planet to the sun, and it takes sunlight about three minutes to reach the surface. Saturn is farther from the sun than Earth is. Sunlight takes over one hour to reach Saturn.

3. Review the first paragraph. Underline facts that support the title of the article.

4. Review the second paragraph. Underline facts that support the title of the article.

5. After reading the paragraphs, what can you infer about the sun's light? Choose the correct answer.

    a. Sunlight takes the same amount of time to reach all the planets.

    b. Sunlight takes longer than one hour to reach Neptune, the farthest planet.

    c. Sunlight does not reach some of the farthest planets.

    d. Sunlight provides the same amount of energy to each planet.

It's a Bird! It's a Plane! It's a Star!

There are many different types of objects in the night sky. Billions of them are stars, but stars are not the only objects in the night sky.

Objects in the Night Sky

6. Look at each picture. As you read about the objects, think about whether they are stars or not. Underline characteristics that can help you decide. Do not write on the lines yet.

Halley's Comet is made of ice, dust, and gases. It can't make its own light. It can be seen about every 75 years when its orbit around the sun brings it close to Earth.

_____

Betelgeuse is around 1,000 times bigger than the sun, but it is not quite as hot with a temperature of 3,226 °C. It is very bright. It is made of gases and produces its own light.

_____

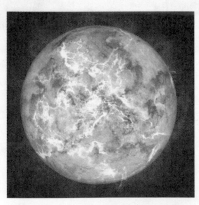

The sun is made mainly of the gases hydrogen and helium. It provides all the light and heat for Earth. Its temperature is about 5,504 °C.

Mars is found in our solar system. It is made of rock and does not produce its own light. It orbits around the sun. It is cooler than Earth.

Vega is made of gases. It produces light and is much brighter than the sun. Its temperature is about 9,500 °C.

_____

_____

_____

243 Ida orbits the sun between Mars and Jupiter. It is small and rocky. It has an irregular shape. 243 Ida does not make its own light.

Bellatrix is a big ball of gases. It is ten times bigger than the sun. The light it gives off is about 4,000 times brighter than sunlight. Its temperature is about 21,726 °C.

_____   _____

7. Look at the properties in the chart. Decide whether each property describes a star or not. Choose the correct answer for each row. The first one is done for you.

Property	Star	Not a star
Made of hot, glowing gases	*	
Made of rock		
Made of ice, dust, and gas		
Has an irregular shape		
Orbits a planet		
Makes its own light		

8. Now add a label to the line under each image. Write "star" or "not a star" under each picture.

Sun Project

9. Use what you have learned and additional research to create a project about the sun. Choose one of the listed projects or choose your own. Use visuals in your project.

Use the lines below to write down facts to include in your presentation.

Projects
- mock webpage
- brochure
- multimedia presentation
- news report
- compose a song
- create a game

_____

_____

_____

_____

_____

_____

EVIDENCE NOTEBOOK Think back to the information you read about the sun. Is the sun a star? Explain your reasoning. Write your thoughts in your Evidence Notebook.

Putting it Together

Scientists use evidence to support their claims about objects in the world. Two types of objects we have discussed are the sun and stars. Is the sun a star? Use evidence to support your claim.

10. Decide if the sun is a star. Choose a claim below.

    a. The sun is a star.

    b. The sun is not a star.

11. Support your claim with evidence. Choose all the evidence statements that apply.

    a. The sun makes its own light.

    b. The sun is made of rock.

    c. The sun is made of gases.

    d. The sun has an irregular shape.

How Does Distance Affect the Size of Objects?

It's a Matter of Perspective

Have you ever seen a large skyscraper in the distance? It looks very small, doesn't it? Your ideas about the size of an object depend on the size of the object and how close you are to it. When you compare the sizes of objects, you are comparing their scale. The skyscraper looked small to you because of its position far in the distance.

12. Why does the airplane in the image appear smaller than the car?

   a. The airplane is a smaller size than the car.

   b. The airplane is farther away from the viewer than the car is.

   c. The airplane is not as shiny as the car, so it is harder to see.

13. Which property best explains why the streetlights in the back of the picture don't look as bright as the streetlights in the front?

   a. They are a different shape.

   b. They are a different size.

   c. They are in the distance.

14. Compare the scale of two other objects in the image.

_____

_____

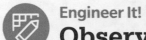
Observing Objects in the Sky

Scientists use telescopes to study objects in space. A telescope collects light to observe distant objects. It makes faraway objects look closer and clearer.

The first telescopes were made of two lenses. Later, scientists began using mirrors in telescopes. Today, the largest telescopes have mirrors that are almost 40 meters in diameter. Other large telescopes orbit Earth and send back images from space.

1609
Galileo Galilei was the first scientist to use a telescope. He observed the moons of Jupiter and the mountains and craters on our own moon. Galileo had an excellent idea for gathering evidence to determine if the sun is a star. However, his telescope was not powerful enough to do this.

1789
Scientist William Herschel built the first large telescope. The telescope tube was 12 meters long, and the mirror was more than 1 meter in diameter. The large mirror allowed Herschel to see much fainter objects than Galileo with his telescope, including huge collections of stars called galaxies and the planet Uranus, which had never been seen before.

15. Which advancement helped telescopes collect more light? Choose the correct answer.

    a. reducing the size of the lenses

    b. building longer telescope tubes

    c. using mirrors instead of lenses

    d. basing telescopes on Earth

1937

Grote Reber, an engineer, built the first radio telescope. This allowed scientists to "see" invisible radio waves. His telescope helped scientists learn about space in a new way.

1990

The European Space Agency helped NASA design the plan for the world's first space telescope. The Hubble Space Telescope orbits above Earth's atmosphere. This allows it to gather clear images.

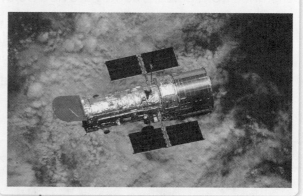

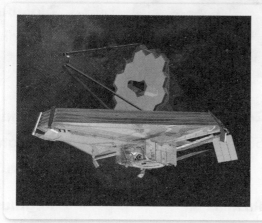

2018

The most powerful telescope in the history is set to launch in 2018. The James Webb Space Telescope is made of ultralight materials and has a sun shield as big as a tennis court. To fit into the rocket that will launch it into space, its main mirror is folded and will open like the petals of a flower once the telescope is in space.

16. What is one advantage of space telescopes over Earth-based telescopes? Choose the correct answer.

   a. Space telescopes are bigger.

   b. Space telescopes use lenses rather than mirrors.

   c. Space telescopes orbit above Earth's atmosphere.

   d. Space telescopes can "see" radio waves.

Light Years

Distances between stars are enormous. If we used units such as kilometers, we would end up with very big numbers. To measure the huge distances in space, scientists use a unit of measurement called a light-year. A light-year is how far light travels in one Earth year. The distance traveled is 9,500,000,000,000 kilometers (9.5 trillion km).

How Far Is That Star?

17. All the stars in a constellation may appear to be the same distance from Earth, but they are not. Below you will find some of the stars that make up the constellation Leo and how far they are from Earth. Use the distances to place the stars on the diagram on the next page. Color each star on the pole that corresponds to its distance from Earth. Then write the name on the line. One has been done for you.

Explore Online

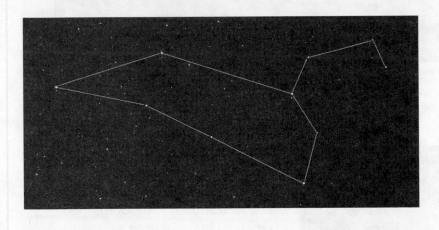

 Algieba
126 light-years

 Adhafera
260 light-years

 Zosma
58 light-years

 Algenubi
250 light-years

 Denebola
36 light-years

 Rasalas
133 light-years

 Regulus
77 light-years

18. Why are distances to stars measured in light-years instead of a familiar unit of distance such as kilometers or miles? Choose the correct answer.

    a. Stars are very far from Earth, so large units are used to measure their distances.

    b. Stars give off light, so light units are used to measure their distances.

    c. It takes a long time to travel to stars, so time units are needed to measure distances to stars.

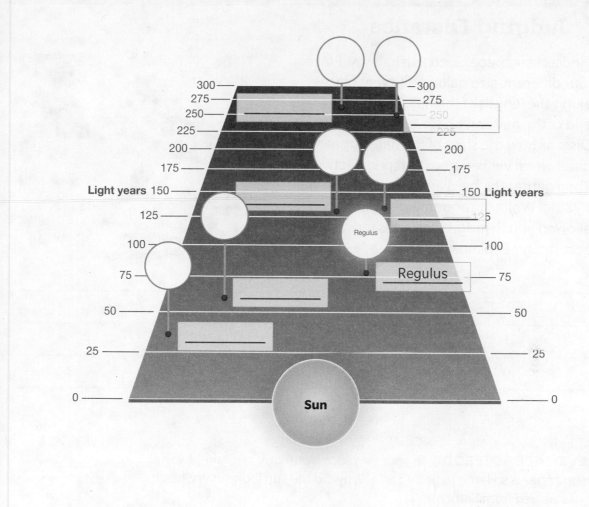

As you can see from the chart, stars vary greatly in their distance from Earth. It would take over a million years to travel to Denebola, which is the closest star shown here!

19. Which statement about stars is true? Choose the correct answer.

    a. They are all the same distance from Earth.

    b. They are closer to Earth than the sun is.

    c. They vary greatly in their distance from Earth.

20. Use the distances in the diagram. Which pair of stars below are the greatest distance apart? Choose the correct answer.

    a. Rasalas and Regulus

    b. Algenubi and Adhafera

    c. Zosma and Regulus

    d. Denebola and Zosma

Judging Distance

21. Find a clear space, such as a hallway. Place four different-size balls in different places along the length of the hall. Stand at one end of the hall and observe the balls. Discuss how the sizes of the balls appear to differ when viewed from that perspective. Then gather the balls and place them side by side. Which arrangement of the balls allowed you to judge their sizes most accurately? Explain your answer.

_____

_____

_____

_____

 EVIDENCE NOTEBOOK In your Evidence Notebook, explain why the sun appears so large to us on Earth. Why did the sun look small when it was viewed from Saturn?

 Language SmArts
Understanding Logical Connections

22. You've learned that your view of an object depends on your perspective, or your location compared to the object. Explain how distance can affect your view of stars.

_____

_____

_____

_____

_____

Tip

The English Language Arts Handbook can provide help with understanding logical connections.

Why Does the Sun Appear So Large and Bright?

Star Light, Star Bright

Star light, star bright, first star I see tonight

You may have heard this nursery rhyme about stars. Even little children notice the brightness of a star. Scientists use the term *luminosity* to describe how bright a star is.

Do the Math

Star Power

23. Look at the table below. It shows the stars' luminosity power, or how bright the stars are. Try to find patterns in the number of zeros when multiplying by the power of 10. Use the patterns to fill in the rest of the table.

Name	Luminosity power	Expression	Standard form
Sun	10^0	1	1
Sirius	10^1	10	10
Arcturus	10^2	10 x 10	
Polaris	10^3	10 x 10 x 10	
Antares	10^4		
Centauri	10^5		

24. How many times brighter is Polaris than the sun? Choose the correct answer.

   a. 10

   b. 100

   c. 1,000

   d. 10,000

25. Why do you think Polaris doesn't appear brighter than the sun to viewers on Earth?

_____

_____

Let It Shine!

Look at the night scene shown here. Notice the difference in the brightness of the stars. Notice, too, the sun setting in the background. How far away from Earth do you think the sun and the other stars are?

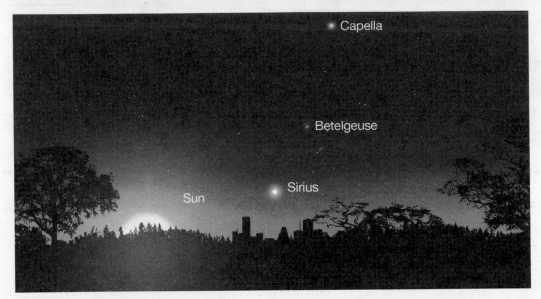

The stars are different distances from Earth. They differ in their brightness, too.

Star	Distance in light-years
Sun	less than 1 ly
Capella	45 ly
Sirius	9 ly
Betelgeuse	520 ly

26. Use the image and chart above to answer the questions.

   a. Write the names of the stars in order from dimmest to brightest as viewed from Earth in the image above.

   b. Write the names of the stars in order from farthest to nearest to Earth.

27. Compare the two diagrams. What pattern do you notice?

The Modest Sun

Distance is one of many things that can affect how bright some stars appear from Earth. The sun appears larger and brighter than the stars shown because it is closer to Earth. Betelgeuse was the farthest and appeared the dimmest from Earth. Look at the image below to see just how large and bright some stars are.

A model of what these stars would look like if they were next to each other.

Can you find the sun in the model above? Look back at the night view of the sky on the opposite page. See how Betelgeuse seems much smaller and dimmer than the sun? In reality, Betelgeuse is around 1,000 times bigger and about 100,000 brighter than the sun. Remember that natural objects exist from the very small to the immensely large.

28. Why did the star Betelgeuse appear to be the dullest when you looked at the picture of it from Earth? Choose the correct answer.

    a. Betelgeuse looks like a bright star because it is farthest from Earth.

    b. Betelgeuse looks like a bright star because it is closest to Earth.

    c. Betelgeuse looks like a dim star because it is farthest from Earth.

    d. Betelgeuse looks like a dim star because it is closest to Earth.

29. What is true of objects in space? Choose the correct answer.

    a. All are smaller than the sun.

    b. They range from small to very large.

    c. They are all extremely small.

    d. Most objects are the same size as Earth.

Blinded by the Light

Try this activity to better understand how we see stars. Copy the chart below onto your paper. Complete each activity listed and record your findings.

ACTIVITY 1 Activate one large and one small glow stick and turn off the lights in the classroom.

ACTIVITY 2 Activate two small glow sticks. Place one close to you and one far away from you.

ACTIVITY 3 Fill the three cups with water, one cold, one room temperature, and one warm. Place one small glow stick in each cup of water. Turn off the lights.

Materials
- 4 glow sticks (one large and three small)
- water
- cups
- thermometers

Activity	Observations	Why did this happen?	How is this similar to stars?
Size			
Distance			
Temperature			

 EVIDENCE NOTEBOOK Is the sun the brightest star there is? If not, why does the sun look so bright to us? Write your ideas in your Evidence Notebook.

 Language SmArts
Providing Evidence

Read the following statement: The sun is the largest and brightest star.

30. Use three to four pieces of evidence to prove that this statement is incorrect. Enter your evidence on the lines below.

_____

_____

_____

_____

Tip

The English Language Arts Handbook can provide help with understanding how to provide evidence.

Find the Light

Objective

Consider This A piece of evidence used to support the idea that the sun is a star came from the invention of the spectroscope—a device that separates the colors in light. The light that a star gives off gives information about the materials that make up the star, such as temperature and what it is made of. By analyzing a star's spectrum, scientists can identify the elements, or parts, that make up the star.

Stars aren't the only light sources that produce spectra. Light bulbs do, too. In this activity, you'll research, design, build, test, and redesign a spectroscope to study the spectra of different kinds of light bulbs. You'll use your observations to identify which light bulb has the spectrum shown in the image on this page.

Collaborate to design, build, and use a spectroscope to identify which light bulb produced the spectrum in the photo.

Find a Problem: What question will you investigate to meet this objective?

_____

_____

_____

_____

Materials
- drawing materials
- CD
- cardboard box
- cardboard tube
- metric ruler
- transparent tape
- packing tape
- glue or tape
- aluminum foil
- dark construction paper
- scissors
- index cards
- lamp
- labeled light bulbs (incandescent, fluorescent)

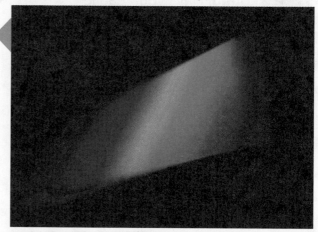

What light bulb made this spectrum?

Criteria

☐ Design a spectrascope to analyze light bulb spectrums.

☐ Determine which light source produced the spectrum in the image.

Constraints

☐ At least half of your materials must be recycled or reused materials.

☐ Spectroscope must be no larger than 38 cm x 38 cm x 38 cm.

Procedure

STEP 1 Research and Brainstorm: Begin by conducting research about how to build a spectroscope. Look over the materials provided by your teacher, and then brainstorm different ideas for your spectroscope. Keep in mind the criteria and constraints.

Why is it important to use accurate science sources for your research?

_____

_____

STEP 2 Plan: Sketch your design. Label all parts.

Does your design meet all the criteria and constraints? How could you revise it to make sure that it does?

_____

_____

STEP 3 Build: Have your teacher review your design. Once approved, build your spectroscope.

STEP 4 Test: Turn on the first labeled light source. Test your design. Then view both light sources with your spectroscope.

Does your design work as planned? Why or why not?

_____

_____

_____

STEP 5 Evaluate and Redesign: Use the results of your test to make improvements to your design.

What changes will you make to improve your design?

_____

_____

Complete the data table as you observe the spectra.

Spectra Data Table	
Type of light bulb	**Description of spectra**

Analyze Your Results

STEP 6 Describe your design. How was it made? What happened when you used it to view a light source?

_____

_____

_____

_____

STEP 7 Communicate: Compare your data with other teams. How was it similar? How was it different?

_____

_____

_____

Draw Conclusions

STEP 8 Make a claim based on your investigation. Provide evidence to support it.

_____

_____

STEP 9 Different light bulbs give off different amounts of light energy, just as different stars give off different amounts of light energy. Knowing this, what can you infer about the temperature of stars that have similar spectra? Cite evidence to support your answer.

_____

_____

Discover More

Check out this path. . . or go online to choose one of these other paths.

People in Science & Engineering

- **Star Colors**
- **Sun Calendars**

William and Margaret Huggins

In the Hands-On Activity, you made a spectroscope. In the late 1800s, two scientists worked together to improve the spectroscope.

William Huggins was born in 1824. He loved science. Around the age of 18, he bought his first telescope. He spent as much time as he could studying the sky.

Margaret (Murray) Huggins was born in 1848. Her grandfather encouraged her love of the stars. She married William Huggins in 1875, and they worked together in his observatory to study the night sky.

William Huggins made a star spectroscope that allowed him to observe distant stars. A spectroscope looks at visible light, or light you can see. He examined the spectra of different objects in space. Margaret Murray worked by his side. They discovered the composition of the sun and other objects. Composition is the materials something is made of.

William Huggins

Margaret Huggins

Huggins' spectroscope

Dr. Beth Brown

Dr. Beth Brown was an astrophysicist. She received a degree in astronomy from the University of Michigan and worked at NASA. One focus of her work was studying galaxies that produce energy in the form of x-rays. To learn about these galaxies, she used data from x-ray telescopes.

Some objects in space give off energy in the form of x-rays, which the human eye can't see. X-ray telescopes are tools that can be used to study these objects. These powerful telescopes are located in space, in an orbit high over Earth! The Chandra X-ray Observatory provides information about the composition, or materials, that make up objects in space.

Dr. Beth Brown

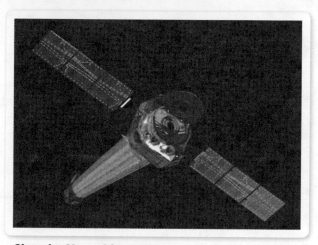

Chandra X-ray Observatory

31. What is a similarity of Huggins' star spectroscope and the spectroscope that is part of the Chandra Observatory? Choose the correct answer.

   a. Both are located on Earth.

   b. Both gather information about visible light.

   c. Both gather data while orbiting Earth.

   d. Both provide data about the composition of objects.

32. Which uses visible light to gather information about objects in space? Choose the correct answer.

   a. the Chandra Observatory

   b. Huggins' star spectroscope

   c. both the Chandra Observatory and Huggins' spectroscope

   d. neither the Chandra Observatory nor the Huggins' spectroscope

Look It Up!

You've read about ways that telescopes and other instruments can be used to gather information about objects in the universe.

33. Now, research 2–3 objects from this list: Vesta, Ganymede, Neptune, Kepler-186f, and Proxima Centauri. Write them on the lines below. Then fill in the table with what you learn.

_____

_____

_____

_____

Object	Discovery date	Characteristics

34. In the space below, make a timeline to show what you learned when researching objects in space.

Lesson Check

Name _____

Can You Explain It?

1. Now that you've learned more about stars and how distance affects our view of an object, explain why the sun looks different on Saturn than it does on Earth. Enter your answer on the lines below. Be sure to do the following:

- Compare the distances between the sun and both Earth and Saturn.
- Describe how greater distance affects the appearance of an object's size and brightness.

 EVIDENCE NOTEBOOK Use the information you've collected in your Evidence Notebook to help you cover each point above.

_____

_____

_____

_____

_____

_____

_____

Checkpoints

2. Choose the best answer. Imagine you are drawing a realistic picture that features both a helicopter and an airplane. You want the helicopter to appear closer to the viewer than the plane. How would you draw the airplane to show it is farther away?

   a. Draw the airplane smaller than the helicopter, with sharp details and bright colors.

   b. Draw the airplane larger than the helicopter with dull colors.

   c. Draw the airplane smaller than the helicopter, with less detail and dull colors.

3. Which is true of the sun? Choose all that apply.

   a. The sun is the closest star to Earth.

   b. The sun is larger than all other stars.

   c. The sun is brighter than all other stars.

   d. The sun is a hot ball of glowing gases.

4. Which statement provides evidence that an object in space is a star?

   a. It orbits Earth.

   b. It is made of rock and dust.

   c. It makes its own light.

   d. It receives and reflects light but does not make light.

5. Choose the correct words to complete each sentence. You can use each word more than once.

> bright   far   hot   dim   close

Luminosity describes how _____ a star is. Stars that

are very luminous can look dim if they are _____ from

Earth. The sun looks very _____ because it is close to

Earth. If the sun were many light-years away from Earth, it would

look _____.

6. Study the diagram. Then choose the correct answer. From which planet would the sun look smallest? Choose the correct answer.

   a. Mars   **c.** Earth

   b. Neptune   **d.** Saturn

Lesson Roundup

A. Write the number of the matching word on each image.

1. Star

2. Not a star

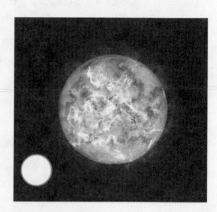

B. Which of the following statements describe the sun? Choose all that apply.
  1. It orbits around another star.
  2. Temperatures on its surface are about 5,500 °C.
  3. It makes its own light.
  4. It is made of gases.

light-year	gravity	megameter
the sun	light	Betelguese

C. To measure the vast distances in space, scientists use a unit called a

_____ , which is how far _____ travels in one year.

The closest star to Earth is _____ .

D. What factors affect how bright a star appears when observed from Earth?
  Choose all that apply.
  1. How bright the star actually is.
  2. How far away the star is.
  3. How many planets orbit the star.

Solar Size

You've been hired by a science museum to create a model for students to observe the properties of stars and the sun. Build a model that shows why the sun appears so large and bright and other stars seem smaller and dimmer.

Why do stars appear to be different sizes?

DEFINE YOUR TASK: What will your model represent?

_____

_____

_____

Before beginning, look at the checklist at the end of this project to be sure you are meeting all the requirements.

RESEARCH: Look back at what you've learned about the sun and stars. Take notes about which information you will use to create your model.

_____

_____

BRAINSTORM: Brainstorm with your team how you will create the model. Keep in mind the requirements below.

Model Requirements

☐ Model demonstrates the differences between star distance

☐ Model demonstrates the differences between star size

☐ Model demonstrates the differences between star brightness

☐ Present your model to the class using information you've learned

☐ Model must be 3D

☐ Presentation must include forms of technology

MAKE A PLAN: Make a plan by considering the questions below.

1. Make a list of needed materials and why you need them.

_____

_____

_____

2. How can you make the stars different brightnesses?

Write down all the details for your plan.

_____

_____

3. How can you make something large appear smaller?

_____

_____

_____

DESIGN AND BUILD: Sketch your design on paper and then build it.

EVALUATE AND REDESIGN: Did you meet the model requirements? What are the ways you could improve your design? Make changes to your model to improve it.

_____

_____

COMMUNICATE: Present your model to your class using technology.

✅ Checklist

Review your project and check off each completed item.

_____ You have met the model requirements

_____ You have built a 3D model

_____ You have answered all the questions on this page

_____ Your presentation included technology

Unit Review

1. You want to prove to someone that Earth is not flat. Which of these pieces of evidence support your claim? Check all that apply.

    a. climbing down into a valley to see more of Earth's surface

    b. climbing to the top of a mountain to see more of Earth's surface

    c. standing on a beach and watching a ship disappear from the horizon

2. Circle the area in the photo where gravity is causing something to fall down.

3. Which of these is an example of gravity?

    a. It pulls everything to the center of Earth.

    b. It pulls everything towards the Southern Hemisphere.

    c. It pulls everything toward the North Pole.

    d. It pulls everything south.

4. Explain the pattern the moon goes through about once a month and what causes that pattern.

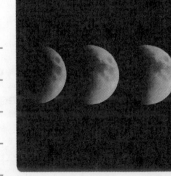

_____

_____

_____

_____

_____

_____

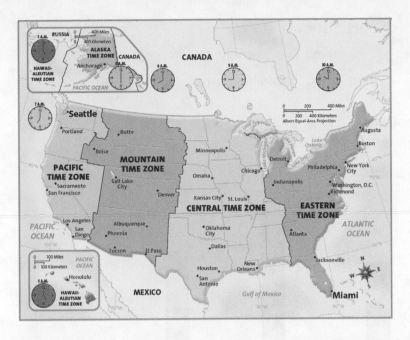

5. Ruby is in Miami and texts her cousin, Xavier, in Seattle. Ruby's clock says 10:00 a.m. When Xavier texts back, he tells her she woke him up. Which of the following is the best explanation as to why Xavier is still in bed? Use the map above to help you answer.

   a. It is 10:00 a.m. in Seattle. Xavier likes to sleep in late.

   b. It is 7:00 a.m in Seattle. The time difference is caused by Earth's daily rotation.

   c. It is 7:00 a.m. in Seattle. The time difference is caused by Earth's revolution around the sun.

   d. It is 4:00 a.m. in Seattle. The time difference is caused by the moon orbiting the Earth.

6. What time of day is the sun at its highest point in the sky?

   a. around sunrise   **c.** around sunset

   b. around noon

7. From Earth, our sun appears larger and brighter than other stars. Explain why by providing two pieces of evidence to support that distance affects how things are seen.

   _____

   _____

   _____

   _____

   _____

8. Which of the following is *not* a characteristic of a star?

   a. made of hot, glowing gases

   b. makes its own light

   c. is extremely hot

   d. orbits the sun

9. The graph below shows the pattern of daylight hours throughout the year. Use the graph below to select the best answer.

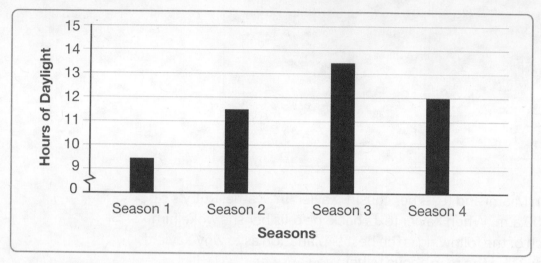

Which season represents the hours of daylight in the summer months of the United States?

   a. season 1   **b.** season 2   **c.** season 3   **d.** season 4

10. Look at the image of the constellation Orion shown in winter.

If you look at the sky at the same time a few months later, in spring, where will Orion be located? Choose the image that shows the correct pattern of movement for Orion.

Earth's Systems

Explore
Online

Unit Project: Cleaning Water
How can you remove salt to make salt water drinkable? You will investigate and design a solution with your team. Ask your teacher for details.

Earth's systems interact. Water from the hydrosphere can shape the land of the geosphere.

At a Glance

Vocabulary Game: Password

Materials
• Kitchen timer or online computer timer

How to Play

1. Take turns to play.

2. To take a turn, choose a word from the Word Box. Do not tell the word to the other players.

3. After choosing a word, set the timer for 1 minute.

4. Give a one-word clue about your word. Point to another player. That player has one chance to guess your word.

5. Repeat step 4 until another player guesses the word, or time runs out. Give a different one-word clue each time.

6. The first player to guess the word gets 1 point. If the player can use the word in a sentence, he or she gets 1 more point. Then that player gets the next turn choosing a word.

7. The first player to score 5 points wins.

biosphere

All the living things on Earth.

geosphere

The solid portion of Earth.

Unit Vocabulary

 **atmosphere:** The mixture of gases that surround a planet.

 **geosphere:** The solid portion of Earth.

 **biosphere:** All the living things on Earth.

 **hydrosphere:** All of Earth's water, taken together in all states of matter.

 **coastline:** The place at which land masses meet the ocean.

 **precipitation:** Water that falls from the air to Earth's surface.

 **condensation:** The process by which a gas changes into a liquid.

 **system:** A set of connected things forming a complex whole.

 **evaporation:** The process by which a liquid changes into a gas.

 **water cycle:** The process in which water continuously moves from Earth's surface into the atmosphere and back again.

What Are Earth's Major Systems?

At Mount Hood in Oregon, you can see four of Earth's systems, which are also known as spheres.

By the end of this lesson . . .
you'll be able to identify and describe each of Earth's systems and the cycles that occur within them.

Can You Explain It?

 Explore Online

Earth's water moves in a cycle. Much of the water that we drink today was on Earth 100 million years ago. That's long enough to have been a dinosaur's thirst quencher. There are other important cycles that take place in Earth's systems.

1. What is a cycle?

_____

_____

_____

_____

_____

_____

_____

_____

_____

Tip

Learn more about what Earth's systems are made of in What Is Matter? and What Are Properties of Matter?

 EVIDENCE NOTEBOOK Look for this icon to help you gather evidence to answer the question above.

Systems and Cycles: Geosphere

Overlapping Spheres

Earth has several systems. A **system** is a collection of parts that interact. Explore the images to learn more about Earth's systems, also known as spheres.

Earth's systems include the geosphere, the atmosphere, the hydrosphere, and the biosphere. Each system has cycles. Interactions among systems affect the planet in different ways.

The **biosphere** contains all living things on Earth. It overlaps with other systems because most organisms live in or on the ground or in the water. The biosphere provides shelter and food and can be cold (the poles) or hot (deserts), wet, swampy, or dry.

The **atmosphere** is made up of all the air that surrounds Earth. One of the ways it overlaps with other systems is because all living things need air in order to live. The atmosphere extends from about 1 meter below Earth's surface to about 10,000 km above it. The lower atmosphere contains the right amount of air for us to breathe.

The **geosphere** contains all the solid land at Earth's surface as well as all the materials that extend to Earth's core. This is by far the most massive system. Interactions between the geosphere and other systems occur at Earth's surface, and often happen very slowly.

The **hydrosphere** contains all Earth's water in all its forms—solid, liquid, and gaseous. The hydrosphere overlaps with other spheres, as water can be found underground, in organisms, and in the atmosphere. Water covers about three quarters of Earth's surface.

2. Choose the correct term to complete each sentence.

| biosphere | hydrosphere | geosphere | atmosphere |

The _____ contains all the water on Earth. All the air

around Earth makes up the _____. Living things make

up the _____. The land at Earth's surface is part of the

_____.

 EVIDENCE NOTEBOOK For each system, write down something in your neighborhood that is part of that system.

Geosphere: The Big Picture

The geosphere consists of four main layers: the crust, the mantle, the outer core, and the inner core.

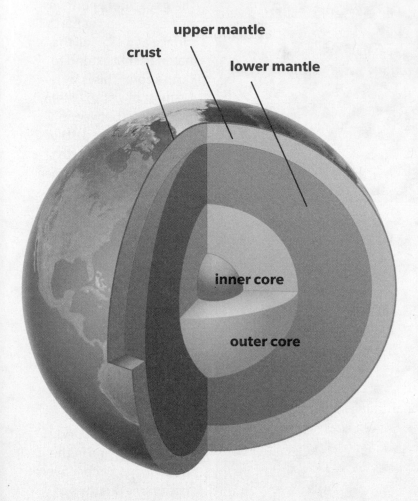

Earth's **crust** is the top layer of the geosphere. It is solid and ranges in depth from 0 km on the ocean floor to 70 km at the top of some mountains. It covers Earth's surface. Temperatures can range from 0 °C to nearly 800 °C close to the mantle.

The **mantle** is below the crust and is divided into an upper layer and a lower layer. The mantle consists of rock that is solid but can flow, and is about 2,900 km thick. Away from boundaries with other layers, the mantle has a temperature of 1,350 °C to 2,500 °C.

The **outer core** is below the mantle, from about 2,900 km to 5,200 km deep. It is a liquid alloy made up mostly of iron and nickel, with a temperature of 4,000 to 5,500 °C.

The **inner core** is at the center of Earth. It is a solid ball of mostly iron and nickel. It is 5,200 km to 6,400 km below Earth's surface, and reaches temperatures between 5,500 °C and 6,200 °C.

3. Fill in the following chart to compare and contrast the characteristics of each layer of the geosphere.

	Crust	Mantle	Outer core	Inner core
Thickness (km)				
State of matter				
Temperature (°C)				
Composition				

Dirt and Soil

You may have noticed that the geosphere changes. Rocks are broken down and moved by wind and water, changing the appearance of Earth's surface. Changes that you can't see also occur below Earth's surface.

4. Study the dirt shown in the photo. What is dirt made of?

_____

_____

_____

_____

_____

_____

If you look closely, you can see that dirt is made of specifically defined particles of sand, silt, and gravel, as well as organic material.

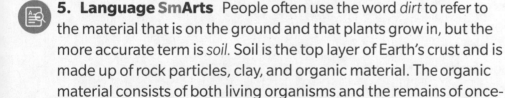

5. Language SmArts People often use the word *dirt* to refer to the material that is on the ground and that plants grow in, but the more accurate term is *soil*. Soil is the top layer of Earth's crust and is made up of rock particles, clay, and organic material. The organic material consists of both living organisms and the remains of once-living organisms. Soil is what plants grow in.

How could you explain the difference between soil and dirt to friends who say they need to get some dirt because they're going to plant some flowers in their garden?

_____

_____

_____

Rock Cycle

The rock cycle is a cycle in which rocks change from one form to another through natural processes. Rocks are always changing. Some processes in the rock cycle happen more quickly than others. Some, such as weathering and erosion, happen at Earth's surface while others, such as heat and pressure, happen deep inside Earth.

Igneous rock is formed as magma cools. It can be broken down into sediment by weathering and erosion. It can also melt back into magma when exposed to high temperatures or change into metamorphic rock when exposed to high temperatures and pressure.

Sedimentary rock forms when sediment is compacted under moderate pressure and exposed to mineral-rich water. It changes into metamorphic rock when exposed to heat and high pressure, and can be broken down into sediment through weathering and erosion.

Metamorphic rock can be broken down into sediment through the processes of weathering and erosion. If exposed to high temperatures, it can melt and then cool and become igneous rock.

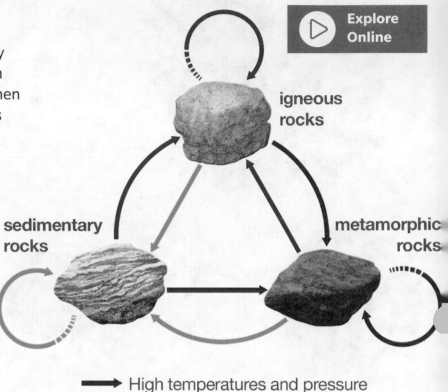

Explore Online

igneous rocks

sedimentary rocks

metamorphic rocks

➡ High temperatures and pressure
➡ Melting and recooling
➡ Breakdown and cementation

Putting It Together

6. How does the rock cycle contribute to the production of soil at Earth's surface?

_____

_____

_____

Atmosphere: The Big Picture

Blanket of Air

Earth's atmosphere is made up of all the air in and around Earth. The atmosphere contains the oxygen we breathe and helps keep temperatures on Earth within a range that allows living things to survive.

The **troposphere** is the layer we live in. It extends about 20 km above Earth's surface. Weather happens there. Also, as altitude (distance from Earth's surface) increases, temperature decreases.

The **stratosphere** is the layer from about 20 km to about 50 km above Earth's surface. It contains the ozone layer, which helps protect Earth from the sun's ultraviolet radiation. Because of the ozone layer, as altitude increases, temperature also increases.

The **exosphere** extends from about 700 km to 10,000 km above Earth's surface. The exosphere is the boundary between Earth's atmosphere and space.

Art is not to scale.

The **mesosphere** extends from about 50 km to 85 km above Earth's surface. It is in the mesosphere that most meteors burn up due to friction with air. As altitude increases, temperature decreases.

The **thermosphere** extends from about 85 km to about 700 km above Earth's surface. In the thermosphere, as altitude increases, temperature also increases.

Do the Math
Measuring Layers

7. Which layer of the atmosphere has the greatest range in distance? Show your calculations.

Pressurized Particles

The pressure that air particles exert on objects is called air pressure. Gravity pulls air particles toward Earth, causing them to squeeze more tightly together near Earth's surface. This results in pressure on objects around and below them, including Earth's surface and you.

You can see this pressure in action when you suck the air from a juice box. The box collapses because of the pressure on it from the atmosphere. Air pressure is lower at higher altitudes in the atmosphere, while it's higher at lower altitudes.

Explore Online

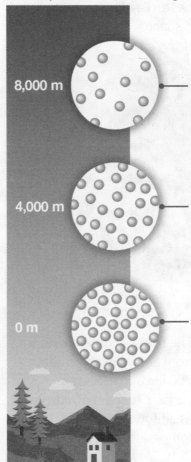

8,000 m

Low Pressure Air particles high in the atmosphere are less tightly packed. If you could see them, they would appear farther apart. These particles do not exert as much pressure as the denser air lower in the atmosphere.

4,000 m

Higher Pressure Air particles in the middle of the atmosphere are more tightly packed than the ones above them. They exert more pressure.

0 m

Highest Pressure Air particles close to Earth's surface are even more tightly packed than the ones above them. They are closer together and exert the most air pressure at Earth's surface.

Putting It Together

8. Describe the relationship between air pressure and altitude. What explains this relationship?

_____

_____

_____

Modeling Earth's Layers

Objective

Collaborate to learn more about the layers in the geosphere. What do you think would be the best way to represent Earth's layers? In this activity, you will make a scale model of Earth's layers.

What question will you investigate to meet this objective?

_____

_____

_____

Materials

- newspaper
- ruler
- 4 colors of modeling clay
- clear, plastic straw
- calculator

Procedure

STEP 1 You will make a model of the geosphere. Use the scale of 1 cm = 1,000 km. Using a calculator, calculate and record the thickness of each layer in your model.

Earth Layer Scale

Layer	Approximate thickness	Model thickness
Crust	30 km	
Mantle	2,900 km	
Outer core	2,300 km	
Inner core	1,200 km	

Why do you need a scale to make a model of the geosphere?

_____

_____

STEP 2 Prepare your workspace. Spread the newspaper across the table. Gather the remaining materials needed.

Why is it important to keep your workspace clean and organized?

_____

_____

_____

_____

STEP 3 Determine which color of modeling clay you will use for each layer. Build the model from the inside out: inner core, outer core, mantle, and crust. Shape the first layer into a round disk. Use the ruler to measure the thickness of the clay so that it is to scale.

Why is it important to make accurate measurements when building your model?

_____

_____

_____

_____

STEP 4 Use the straw to take a sample of your model. Place the straw over the center of your model, and press it down into the clay to the bottom of the model. Remove the straw. Draw a picture of your sample in your Evidence Notebook.

How does taking a sample with the straw help you visualize the layers in your model?

_____

_____

_____

_____

Analyze Your Results

STEP 5 By examining your model only, what inferences could a person make about the thickness of each of Earth's layers in relation to the others?

_____

_____

STEP 6 Scientists sometimes make life-size models of things. Why was it necessary for you to make a scale model as opposed to a life-size model?

_____

_____

STEP 7 Scientists often refine their models to increase accuracy. Was the thickness of your crust layer as accurate as it could be? What other materials might you use to refine your model?

_____

_____

Draw Conclusions

STEP 8 Scientists have not yet been able to drill to the mantle. Make a claim about why drilling through Earth's crust might be so challenging. Cite evidence to support your claim.

_____

_____

_____

_____

STEP 9 Earth is round, but your model is flat. How could you change it to more closely resemble Earth?

_____

_____

STEP 10 How could you use your model to explain what the geosphere is to a younger sibling or classmate?

_____

_____

Systems and Cycles: Hydrosphere and Biosphere

Blue Planet

The hydrosphere includes all the water on Earth, including ice, snow, liquid water, and water vapor, which is water in a gaseous state. Earth is often referred to as the "blue planet." Look at the photo below and consider this nickname.

9. Why is Earth so blue?

_____

_____

_____

_____

_____

About 70% of Earth's surface is covered with water. The oceans contain most of that water, which means that most of the planet's water is salt water. The rest is considered fresh water.

Lakes, rivers, and streams contain a small percentage of Earth's fresh water. Other examples found on Earth's surface include snow, ice, and pools of rain or snowmelt.

Most of the water on Earth is found in oceans, or the large bodies of water that separate most continents. Ocean water is different from fresh water because it contains salt.

A large amount of Earth's fresh water is contained in glaciers, icebergs, and the ice sheets that cover Antarctica and parts of the Arctic.

The remaining fresh water is located underground and is called groundwater. Like fresh surface water, people use groundwater as a source of drinking water.

10. Choose the best terms to complete the sentences below.

> **fresh water**   **salt water**   **gaseous**   **liquid**   **solid**   **oceans**

Lakes, rivers, and streams are all examples of _____ found

on Earth's surface. Glaciers and ice sheets are examples of water in a

_____ state. Most of the water on Earth is in _____.

Groundwater is fresh water that is found _____.

🖐 **HANDS-ON Apply What You Know**

Water Fresh and Salty

11. Pour 1 liter of water into a container. This represents all the water on Earth. Add 4 drops of food coloring to the container and stir. Pour 28 mL of water from the container into a graduated cylinder. This represents all of the fresh water on Earth. Pour 7 mL of the 28 mL of water into another graduated cylinder. This represents all of the non-frozen fresh water on Earth. Study how much water is in each container. Do you think it is important to protect and conserve fresh water on Earth? Why or why not?

_____

_____

_____

Water Beneath Our Feet

Much of the world's liquid fresh water is underneath our feet in large stores of groundwater.

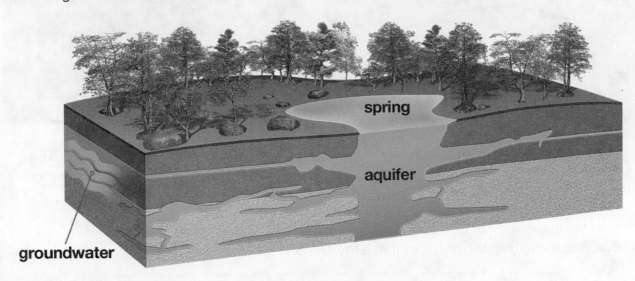

groundwater
spring
aquifer

There are small spaces between particles of rock underground. Water fills in these spaces. At a certain depth, the ground becomes saturated—it cannot hold any more water. Sometimes water can accumulate into an underground layer of groundwater called an aquifer. People drill wells into aquifers to pump this water to the surface for use. When precipitation falls to Earth's surface and sinks into the ground, the aquifer can be replenished.

 12. Language SmArts When you talk about water in everyday life, you're probably talking about the liquid water that you use to drink, cook, and water plants. When scientists talk about water, they are usually more specific, using terms such as fresh water, groundwater, salt water, water vapor, or glaciers. In the context of science, water is a substance made of hydrogen and oxygen.

Why do you think it is important for scientists to use specific terms when talking about water?

_____

_____

_____

 EVIDENCE NOTEBOOK What do you use water for? What are other uses of water? Do you think it is important to keep water free from pollution? Why? Write your answers in your Evidence Notebook.

The Living Sphere

The biosphere is all the living things on Earth, from the smallest microscopic organism to the largest animal—the blue whale.

13. Compare this photo to the picture shown at the beginning of the lesson. What can you infer about the biosphere from these?

_____

_____

_____

The biosphere can be organized into different parts. An individual organism is the smallest level. A population is all the individuals of the same species living in an area at the same time. A community is a group of different populations living in an area at the same time.

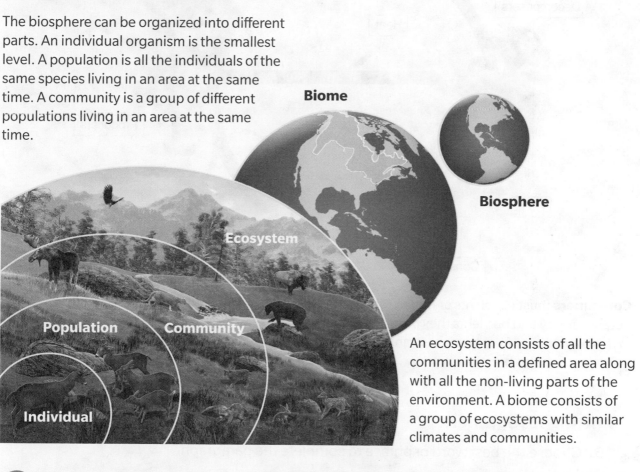

An ecosystem consists of all the communities in a defined area along with all the non-living parts of the environment. A biome consists of a group of ecosystems with similar climates and communities.

14. Language SmArts Organizing large systems such as the biosphere into smaller parts can help scientists determine how systems function. What analogy can you make using a different example of a system that is organized from largest to smallest?

_____

_____

_____

Biosphere: Energy-Matter Cycle

Organisms in the biosphere are dependent on each other. Their interactions contribute to a cycle of energy and matter.

Decomposers recycle materials in ecosystems. This releases nutrients and organic matter for other organisms to use.

Producers such as plants use the **nutrients** provided by decomposers as part of photosynthesis, continuing the cycle of matter and energy.

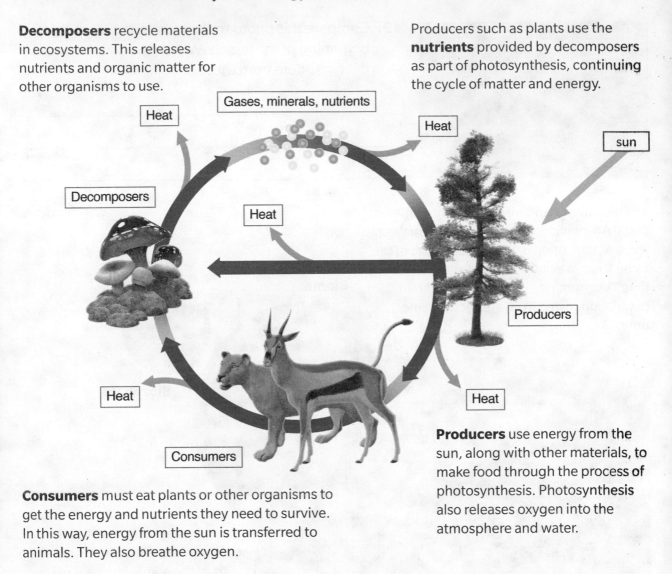

Gases, minerals, nutrients

Heat

Heat

sun

Decomposers

Heat

Producers

Heat

Heat

Consumers

Consumers must eat plants or other organisms to get the energy and nutrients they need to survive. In this way, energy from the sun is transferred to animals. They also breathe oxygen.

Producers use energy from the sun, along with other materials, to make food through the process of photosynthesis. Photosynthesis also releases oxygen into the atmosphere and water.

Putting It Together

15. Choose the best word or phrase to complete the paragraph.

the sun	nutrients	decomposers	energy

Plants use energy from _____ to carry out photosynthesis. When animals eat plants or other organisms, they get the nutrients and _____ they need to survive. When organisms die, _____ break down their bodies and release _____ and matter back into the environment.

Discover More

Check out this path . . . or go online to choose one of these other paths.

Careers in Science & Engineering

- **Model Earth: Above and Below**
- **Caves**

Volcanologist

Imagine being so close to a volcano that you can feel the heat and smell the smokey air. You might be able to see lava flowing. You are there to collect data as part of your job as a volcanologist. Volcanologists are scientists who study volcanoes. They collect and study data to learn more about volcanoes and how to predict when they might erupt.

Explore Online

A volcanologist can set up instruments that will record measurements of gases and movement around an active volcano, to predict when an eruption is likely to take place. This volcanologist is watching the lava churn from a safe viewing area above the action.

A volcanologist's duties may include analyzing rock samples from a volcano, photographs of a volcano, gases emitted by a volcano, and movements of rock near the volcano. A volcanologist may work for the government of a country or a university.

This robot, developed by NASA, explores cracks in volcanoes that are too small for humans to venture into. It sends video and other data back to the surface in real time.

The area of Earth that surrounds the Pacific Ocean is known as the "Ring of Fire" because of the number of volcanoes it features.

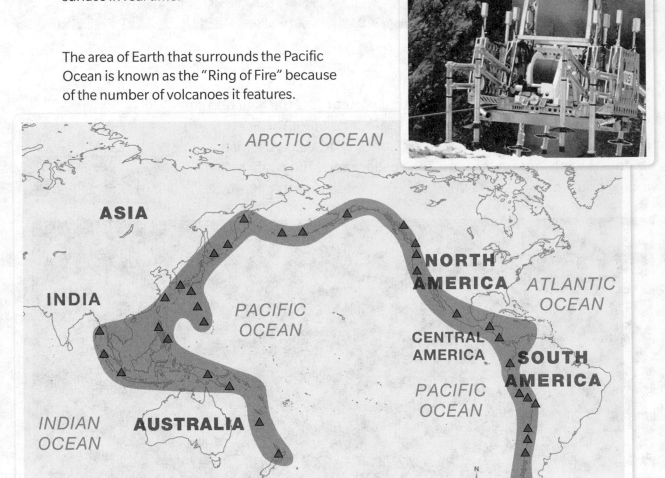

▲ Volcano

km 0   2,000
mi 0   2,000

16. Why do you think it is important for scientists to study volcanoes?

_____

_____

_____

Lesson Check

Name _____

Can You Explain It?

1. Now that you've learned more about Earth's systems and the cycles that occur in them, identify and explain two of the cycles. For each cycle, be sure to:

   • Identify in which system the cycle occurs.

   • Explain the cycle.

   • Explain why the cycle is important.

Explore Online

EVIDENCE NOTEBOOK Use the information you've collected in your Evidence Notebook to help you cover each point.

_____

_____

_____

_____

_____

_____

_____

_____

_____

_____

Checkpoints

2. Which statement about groundwater is true?

   a. Groundwater is the water found between particles of rock below Earth's surface.

   b. Groundwater makes up the largest portion of fresh water on Earth.

   c. Groundwater is mostly salt water.

   d. Groundwater is not used as drinking water.

3. Match each layer of the geosphere with its description.

> inner core   outer core   mantle   crust

_____ top layer of geosphere, solid, depth varies from 5 km to 30 km

_____ solid ball of iron, reaches temperatures between 5,500 °C and 6,200 °C

_____ semisolid rock with a temperature of about 1,200 °C

_____ liquid iron and nickel heated to about 5,000 °C

4. Place the name for each layer of the atmosphere on the diagram.

> exosphere   mesosphere   stratosphere   thermosphere   troposphere

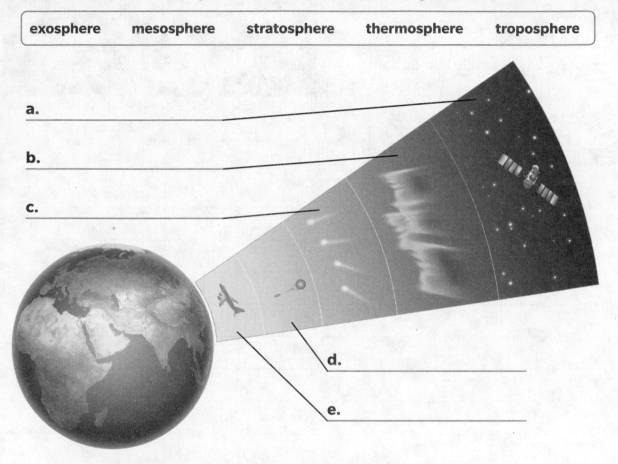

a. _____

b. _____

c. _____

d. _____

e. _____

5. Which represents the largest percentage of fresh water on Earth?
  a. glaciers, ice sheets, and icebergs   **c.** lakes, rivers, and streams
  b. groundwater   **d.** oceans

6. Which list represents the correct organization of the biosphere from smallest to largest?
  a. biosphere, biome, ecosystem, community, population, individual
  b. biome, biosphere, community, ecosystem, individual, population
  c. individual organism, population, community, ecosystem, biome, biosphere
  d. population, individual, community, biome, ecosystem, biosphere

Lesson Roundup

A. A volcano on the ocean floor erupts. Magma from the mantle flows up through the crust as hot lava. The lava cools and hardens into volcanic rock. Over time, the buildup of new rock produces an island, and the opening of the volcano can be seen high above the sea surface. What type of rock is the volcano made of?

   a. igneous

   b. metamorphic

   c. sedimentary

....

B. Which is true about air pressure? Circle all that apply.

   a. As altitude increases, air pressure increases.

   b. As altitude increases, air pressure decreases.

   c. As altitude increases, the density of air increases

   d. As altitude increases, the density of air decreases.

....

C. A farmer drills a well on his land. He uses the water he pumps from the well to water his crops. He has drilled his well into _____ .

   a. an aquifer.   **c.** the ozone layer.

   b. the biosphere.   **d.** the stratosphere.

....

D. Choose the correct words to complete the sentences.

weathering	**photosynthesis**	**erosion**	**energy**
water	**decomposers**	**animals**	**plants**

Plants use energy from the sun to carry out _____. Animals

must eat plants or other animals to get the _____ and

nutrients they need to survive. When animals and other organisms die,

_____ break down their bodies and release nutrients into

the environment.

387

How Do Earth's Systems Interact?

How do Earth systems affect each other? In what ways do living things, solid Earth, the atmosphere, and Earth's water interact?

By the end of this lesson . . .
you'll be able to describe how Earth's systems interact.

Can You Explain It?

 Explore Online

Our food comes from interactions among Earth's systems. The biosphere includes the farmer and plants. Water used by the plants is part of the hydrosphere. Plants grow in soil, which is part of the geosphere. Plants absorb and give off gases that are part of the atmosphere.

1. How do you think Earth's systems are interacting in the image?

_____

_____

_____

_____

_____

_____

_____

Tip

Learn more about Earth's systems in What Are Earth's Major Systems?.

 EVIDENCE NOTEBOOK Look for this icon to help you gather evidence to answer the question above.

How the Atmosphere and Hydrosphere Interact

Cycling and Recycling

The water cycle involves all of Earth's systems. It takes place all over Earth, and it involves a variety of different processes.

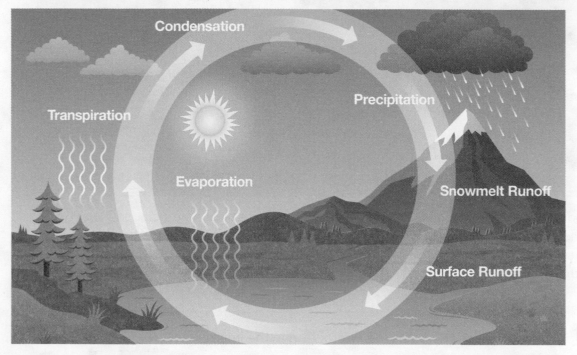

Remember that a cycle is something that repeats over and over in a pattern. In the **water cycle,** water moves among and between Earth's systems. It changes forms and locations. There are many different paths that water can take through the water cycle.

2. The main processes of the water cycle are evaporation, condensation, and precipitation. Name one feature in the diagram that is most directly related to each process.

_____

_____

_____

 EVIDENCE NOTEBOOK In your Evidence Notebook, identify ways that Earth's systems interact in the water cycle. Be sure to consider all four major Earth systems in your response.

What Goes Up . . .

Water on Earth changes form and location by moving through the water cycle. As water moves through the cycle, it interacts with all of Earth's spheres. Several of the changes it undergoes in the water cycle demonstrate how the hydrosphere and atmosphere interact. **Evaporation** is the process by which a liquid changes to a gas. **Condensation** is the process by which a gas changes to a liquid. **Precipitation** is water that falls from clouds to Earth's surface.

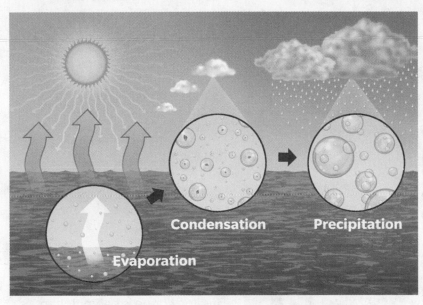

Condensation   Precipitation

Evaporation

a. Evaporation is a process that requires energy. In the water cycle, the sun's energy causes water to evaporate, or change from a liquid to a gas. Here, water is evaporating from the ocean.

b. As water vapor rises into the atmosphere, it loses some energy and condenses, or changes back to a liquid. Particles of water clump together around particles of dust, forming droplets.

c. Inside clouds, water droplets combine to form raindrops that fall to Earth.

Do the Math
How Big Is a Drop?

3. How do the sizes of raindrops, dust particles, and water droplets compare? One way to compare the size of these objects is by ordering fractions. When you order fractions, you place them in sequence.

A water droplet is 1/100 the size of a rain drop. A dust particle is 1/1000 the size of a water droplet. The table shows the size of droplets and dust particles in relation to the size of raindrops. Order the fractions in the table, starting with the fraction that has the smallest value at the top.

Fractions	Ordered Fractions
1/100	
1/1	
1/1000	
1/10	

Case Study: Water and Air Pollution Affects All the Spheres

You've learned that water moves through all of Earth's spheres. As it moves through the water cycle, there are many chances for it to become polluted. Look at the images to see how human actions can affect Earth's water.

This electrical energy generating station burns fossil fuels to produce the electricity people use. Notice that pollution is being released into the atmosphere.

In the short term, acid rain discolors buildings and statues. This lion statue is beginning to show the effects from acid rain.

In the long term, acid rain wears away even the hardest brick and stone. The detail in the lion's face is nearly gone after decades of exposure to acid rain.

Look at the images below to see how pollution can spread through water.

This rainwater has become polluted. As it moves into the storm drain, the pollution is carried along with it.

The polluted rainwater enters a body of water. Now the pollution could affect the entire body of water and all the living things in and around it.

HANDS-ON **Apply What You Know**

Pollution in Action

4. Food dye can be used to model pollution. Take a teaspoon or dropper of food dye, and add it to a cup of tap water. Observe what happens. Now pour the contents of that cup into a larger container of water. What happens?

_____

_____

Putting It Together

5. Trees are part of the biosphere. They need water to survive. They take in water from the soil through their roots and release water vapor into the air from their leaves. Explain how this shows an interaction of all four of Earth's spheres.

_____

_____

_____

_____

_____

What Happens During the Water Cycle?

Objective

Collaborate to study the influence of oceans on the water cycle.

What question will you investigate to meet this objective?

_____

_____

_____

Materials
- 2 plastic containers
- modeling clay
- measuring spoons
- measuring cup
- salt
- water
- dropper
- plastic wrap
- 2 rubber bands
- 2 small weights

Procedure

STEP 1 Label the plastic containers *A* and *B*. Make two identical clay landform models. Include a lake made out of clay in each model. You will be adding water to the lake in the next step.

Why do you think it is important that the landform models be identical?

_____

STEP 2 Place the landform models on one end of each container. Each model should take up about ¼ of the space in its container. Add 3 drops of fresh water to the lake in A and B. Stir 2 teaspoons of salt into 2 cups of water until the salt dissolves. Pour the salt water into the empty area in container A. Container *B* will not have salt water.

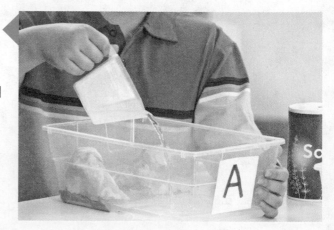

How is the water in the model lakes different from the water in the model oceans?

_____

_____

STEP 3 Cover both containers with plastic wrap. Use a large rubber band to hold the plastic wrap in place.

Why is the plastic wrap important?

_____

_____

_____

STEP 4 Place a small weight on the plastic wrap directly above the land in each model. Place both containers on a sunny windowsill. Two hours later, observe the models and record your observations.

Why is it important to place the model in a sunny area?

_____

_____

Analyze Your Results

STEP 5 After two hours, how did the amount of moisture on the underside of the plastic wrap compare in the two models?

_____

_____

STEP 6 Did you notice any change in the amount of water in the model lakes? If so, what caused the change?

_____

_____

_____

Draw Conclusions

STEP 7 Make a claim about why there were differences between the two models. Cite evidence to support your claim.

_____

_____

_____

How the Atmosphere and Geosphere Interact

The Sun's Energy and Earth

If you step outside on a sunny day, you can feel the warmth of the sun's light. Earth's cycles and the processes associated with them rely on the sun's energy. The sun's energy moves outward in all directions. A tiny part of the sun's total energy affects Earth's spheres.

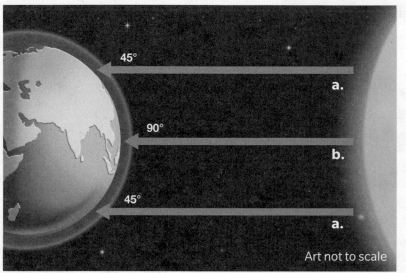

Art not to scale

a. At some locations, the sun's rays do not hit Earth straight on. They strike at an angle. In these places, the energy is spread out over a bigger area. These areas are cooler.

b. Near the equator, the sun's rays strike Earth at a 90° angle. The energy does not spread out. These areas are warmer because more energy is focused on a smaller area.

The sun has an essential role in the water cycle. Recall that evaporation occurs due to energy from the sun. Do the activity below to find out more about how energy from the sun reaches Earth.

 HANDS-ON Apply What You Know

Let It Shine!

6. Place a large sheet of black paper on a flat surface. Place two thermometers on the paper, one in the center and one near the edge. Place a desk lamp above the thermometer in the center of the paper. Measure the distance from the center thermometer to the other thermometer, and record the measurement. Turn on the lamp. Notice how the light strikes each of the thermometers. After three minutes, record the temperature on each thermometer. How did the distance from the center affect the angle at which light struck the thermometer? How does this model the way in which light strikes Earth?

Not all of the sun's energy that moves toward Earth strikes Earth's surface.

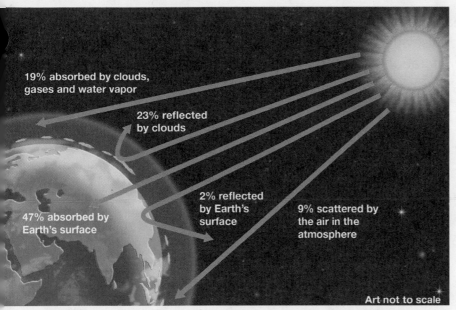

19% absorbed by clouds, gases and water vapor

23% reflected by clouds

2% reflected by Earth's surface

9% scattered by the air in the atmosphere

47% absorbed by Earth's surface

Art not to scale

a. About 9% of the sun's energy is reflected by particles in the atmosphere; another 23% is reflected by clouds.

b. 2% of the sun's energy reaches Earth's surface but then is reflected by features such as ice and snow.

c. About 47% of the sun's energy is absorbed by Earth's surface. About 19% is absorbed by the atmosphere and clouds.

7. Language SmArts Summarize the information about the sun's energy and Earth by stating a main idea and two supporting details about the topic.

_____

_____

_____

_____

_____

8. Choose the correct words to complete each sentence.

| warmer | cooler | all | about half | precipitation | evaporation |

Places where the sun's energy strikes straight on are _____ than places where the sun strikes at a lesser angle. About 25% of the sun's energy that reaches Earth is reflected by clouds, the atmosphere, and Earth's surface. _____ of the sun's energy is absorbed by Earth's surface. In the water cycle, the process of _____ is fueled by the sun's energy.

Where the Wind Blows

When the sun's energy heats Earth, it provides the energy that powers the water cycle. Winds also affect the water cycle. Wind over a body of water can increase evaporation and lead to precipitation.

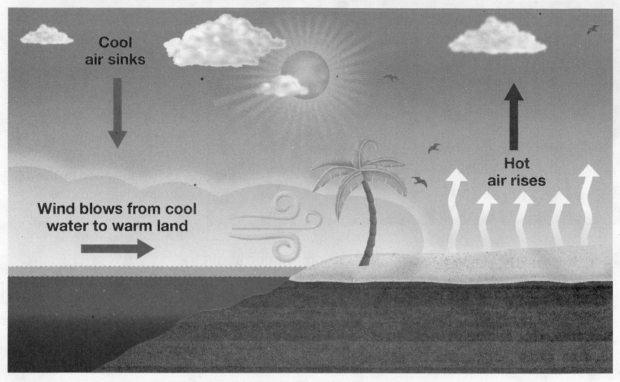

Cool air sinks

Hot air rises

Wind blows from cool water to warm land

Warm air near the equator rises in the atmosphere. Cool air from areas closer to the poles flows toward the equator to fill the void left by the rising warm air. This movement of air is wind. Wind also forms because of temperature differences over land and water. Land heats up and cools down more quickly than water. On a sunny day, air over the land warms and rises, and cooler air over the water flows inland, creating a "sea breeze."

9. Explain how winds are related to the water cycle.

_____

_____

_____

_____

 EVIDENCE NOTEBOOK In your Evidence Notebook, identify an effect of the uneven heating of land and air on Earth.

Case Study—Rain Shadows Affect All the Spheres

You've learned that Earth's spheres affect one another. Look at the images and think about how these pictures show a connection between the geosphere, hydrosphere, and atmosphere.

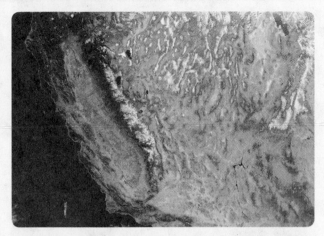

The Sierra Nevada mountain range in the western United States is about 400 km long. This landform is a part of the geosphere that affects the atmosphere and the hydrosphere.

Death Valley is the driest part of the United States. Its average rainfall is less than 5 cm per year! Why is it so dry? And how does this affect the living things in Death Valley?

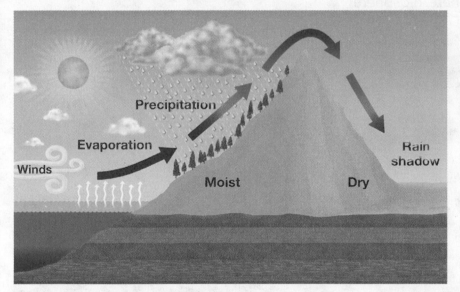

Winds carry moist air from the Pacific Ocean inland toward the Sierra Nevada. As the moist air rises up the west side of the mountains, it cools. The water vapor condenses. Rain and snow fall west of the mountains. When the air goes down the other side of the mountains, it contains very little water. The dry side is called a rain shadow because it gets very little rain. Death Valley is in a rain shadow.

Putting It Together

10. Explain how rain shadows illustrate the interactions of all four of Earth's spheres.

_____

_____

_____

_____

The Atmosphere, Geosphere, and Hydrosphere Shape Earth

Agents of Change: Wind, Water, Ice, and Organisms

Weathering and erosion are processes that cause changes to the geosphere. Recall that weathering is the breaking down of rocks on Earth's surface into smaller pieces. Erosion is the process of moving sediment from one place to another.

What are some causes of weathering and erosion? View the images to explore how weathering and erosion demonstrate interactions between Earth's spheres. Look for examples of interactions between the geosphere and the atmosphere, biosphere, and hydrosphere.

Paria Canyon was formed mostly by weathering and erosion caused by wind. This canyon, located near the border of Arizona and Utah, is home to many beautiful sandstone formations.

The Grand Canyon was formed by the flowing water of the Colorado River. As the water flowed over the rocks in the area, weathering occurred. The moving water broke the rock into smaller pieces and eroded, or moved, it.

A lot of the fresh water on Earth is frozen in glaciers, which are giant sheets of ice. Glaciers move slowly over Earth's surface, causing weathering and erosion. These grooves in Earth's surface were formed as glaciers dragged rocks along the surface.

Living things also cause weathering. This tree is one example. As the tree grows, its roots break apart, or weather, the rock. Some vines can cause weathering by climbing up rock walls and extending roots into small pores and cracks. As the roots grow, the rock can break.

11. Fill in the chart to show how weathering and erosion can affect Earth's spheres.

Sphere	Effects of weathering and erosion
Atmosphere	
Biosphere	
Geosphere	
Hydrosphere	

 EVIDENCE NOTEBOOK In your Evidence Notebook, describe examples of weathering and erosion in the schoolyard or around your neighborhood.

Natural Disasters Affect the Spheres

Volcanoes are a part of the geosphere. A volcanic eruption starts in the geosphere but can affect all of Earth's spheres.

When a volcano erupts, lava flows out of it after moving through the crust as magma, or melted rock. Hot gases and ash are also ejected from the volcano. How do these products of an eruption affect the atmosphere and biosphere?

Gases and particles from the volcano mix with the atmosphere. The gases can affect the way sunlight is reflected by the atmosphere. The particles can block incoming sunlight. Volcanic eruptions can have a major impact on the weather.

Volcanic eruptions can also impact the biosphere. Plants and animals can be affected by lava and ash. Eruptions can also cause long-term changes in nearby soils. Deposits of volcanic material make rich soil that's good for growing some types of plants.

12. Describe ways that volcanic eruptions affect the biosphere. Consider also how an impact on the atmosphere could in turn affect the biosphere.

_____

_____

_____

_____

Case Study—Soil

The geosphere includes the rocks and soil that cover Earth's surface. Recall that soil is made of bits of weathered rock mixed with once-living materials. Air and water are also found in soil. The formation of soil is a great example of a process that involves all four spheres of Earth.

3,000 years ago

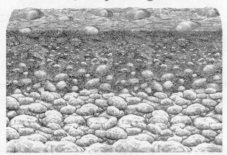

Weathered bits of rock, remains of once-living things, air, and water are all found in soil. Weathering of rocks can occur due to interactions of the geosphere with the biosphere, the atmosphere, or the hydrosphere.

500 years ago

For example, plant roots can break apart rocks. Wind blowing over the surface of rocks can weather and erode rocks. Water that gets into cracks in rocks can freeze and thaw, breaking apart rocks.

Today

The weathered bits of rock mix with the remains of once-living things, air, and water to form soil. When plants grow in the soil, they too die, and parts of them mix with the soil.

Language SmArts
Cause and Effect

13. Describe a cause-and-effect relationship among at least two of Earth's spheres that leads to soil formation. Make sure to use language that clearly connects a specific cause and effect.

_____

_____

_____

_____

Tip

The English Language Arts Handbook can provide help with understanding cause and effect.

How the Biosphere, Geosphere, and Atmosphere Interact

Carbon and Nitrogen Cycles

Matter cycles through Earth's spheres. It moves among the spheres and is combined and recombined in different ways. Recall that water moves among Earth's spheres through the water cycle. The sun provides energy to the water cycle. Energy is vital to the cycles of matter.

The carbon cycle shown is important to the biosphere. But a larger version of the carbon cycle also impacts gases in the atmosphere, the weathering of rocks of the geosphere by those gases, and the particles that end up in oceans of the hydrosphere.

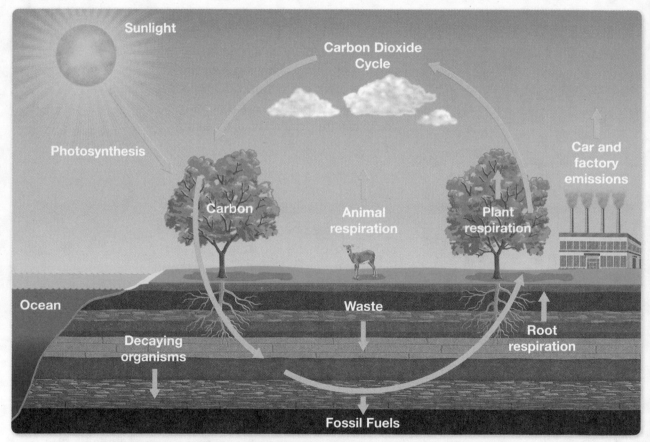

a. During photosynthesis, producers use energy from sunlight to change carbon dioxide and water into food. Consumers get energy when they eat the producers or other consumers.

b. Living things release carbon dioxide during respiration, when they break down food molecules to release the matter and energy in them. Carbon dioxide is a waste product of respiration.

c. Carbon is found in living things. When organisms die, decomposers help break them down. Their bodies may not decompose completely. Instead, they are changed over time into fossils or fossil fuels.

d. When fossil fuels are burned, the carbon and energy in the fossil fuels are released. Carbon that is released during the burning of fossil fuels enters the atmosphere.

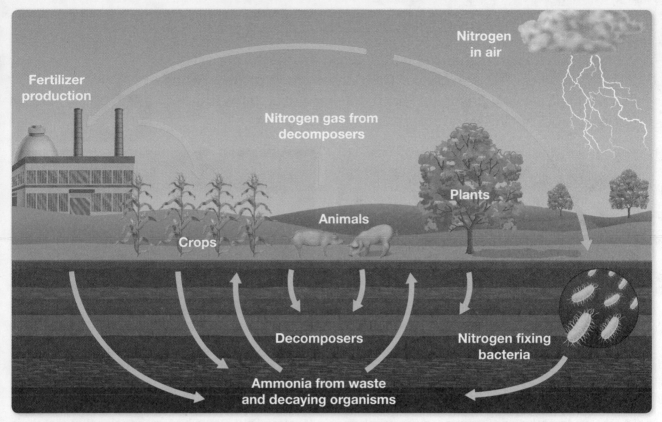

a. Lightning and bacteria can change nitrogen in the atmosphere to a form that can be used by living things through a process called fixation.

b. Plants use nitrogen. When animals eat plants, they absorb some of that nitrogen, and it becomes a part of the animals' bodies.

c. Humans can affect the nitrogen cycle by producing and using nitrogen-containing fertilizers needed by plants for growth.

d. Decomposers release nitrogen back into the soil, providing the nutrition for plants.

14. Choose the correct words to complete each sentence.

taken in	released by	fossil fuels	food molecules
producers	decomposers	make	fix

Respiration is a process that results in carbon being _____ by

organisms. Carbon in the atmosphere taken in by plants can be used in

the formation of _____ during the process of photosynthesis.

Carbon and nitrogen in the remains of once-living things is released by the

action of _____. Bacteria play a key role in the nitrogen cycle

when they _____ nitrogen.

Case Study—Glen Canyon Dam

Humans are a part of the biosphere. Human actions can impact all of Earth's spheres. The Glen Canyon Dam is an example of the ways in which human activities influence Earth's spheres and systems. There are advantages and disadvantages to all human activities.

 Explore Online

The Glen Canyon Dam in Arizona produces hydroelectric energy for many people. It helps prevent flooding of the Colorado River by controlling how much water flows downstream. Construction of the dam decreased the number of fish in the river and permanently changed the movement of sediment in the Colorado River.

Lake Powell was formed by the construction of Glen Canyon Dam. It stores water that is released in a controlled way during droughts. Recent droughts have resulted in extremely low water levels in Lake Powell. Many species that lost their habitat when the dam was built. Lake Powell also affects long term weather patterns in Utah.

15. What are some advantages of the Glen Canyon Dam and Lake Powell? What are some disadvantages?

_____

_____

_____

_____

Putting It Together

16. Provide evidence to support the argument that organisms in the biosphere affect all of Earth's spheres.

_____

_____

_____

_____

_____

Discover More

Check out this path . . . or go online to choose one of these other paths.

Measuring
Weather
Across the
Spheres

- Monsoons
- Agricultural Engineering

Measuring Weather Across the Spheres

When you think of weather, you might think of the conditions right outside your door. But weather happens all around Earth. Weather is the result of the interactions of Earth's spheres.

To prepare weather forecasts and to warn people of possible hazardous weather, scientists need to gather data about the weather all around Earth—not just on land, but in locations over the oceans as well. They also need to know about conditions high up in the atmosphere. The data are analyzed and combined to help scientists understand how Earth's spheres interact and to predict upcoming weather.

A weather station buoy is a technology used to gather data on the ocean. Weather station buoys collect and record data about air temperature, wind speed, wave heights, and air pressure.

Satellites orbit Earth. Some are equipped to gather data about weather conditions, such as cloud cover. They are also used to gather data about the paths of large storms. These bits of information are transmitted back to Earth, where they can be analyzed.

Weather balloons are used to carry technology called *radiosondes*. A radiosonde measures weather factors such as air temperature, air pressure, and the amount of water in the air, or humidity.

Technology is also used to gather weather data on land. Weather stations gather information about conditions such as air temperature and pressure, and they measure and record precipitation. Some use radar to gather data.

17. Think about what you've learned about Earth's systems and how they interact. Use one or more specific things you've learned as evidence to support an argument that many different technologies in many different locations are required to develop a good understanding of weather conditions on Earth.

_____

_____

_____

_____

Lesson Check

Name _____

Can You Explain It?

1. Now that you've learned more about Earth's spheres, explain what you see in the image as an interaction of all four spheres. Be sure to do the following:

Explore Online

- Identify the four spheres of Earth.

- Describe how each of the spheres is involved with growing crops.

- Identify and describe one specific interaction of spheres.

EVIDENCE NOTEBOOK Use the information you've collected in your Evidence Notebook to help you answer these questions.

_____

_____

_____

_____

_____

_____

_____

_____

_____

_____

Checkpoints

2. Which best describes a rain shadow? Circle the correct answer.

   a. a location that receives very little rain due to mountains or hills blocking winds

   b. an area where the sun's rays strike Earth directly, leading to lots of evaporation

   c. a location where rain causes a great amount of erosion, resulting in moisture in the atmosphere

3. Which of these processes are directly involved in the water cycle?
Circle all that apply.

    a. evaporation   **d.** weathering

    b. erosion   **e.** precipitation

    c. condensation

4. Which best describes the interaction shown in this image?
Circle the correct answer.

    a. the atmosphere   **c.** the hydrosphere
       affecting the hydrosphere   affecting the biosphere

    b. the biosphere   **d.** the geosphere
       affecting the geosphere   affecting the atmosphere

5. Which of these explain(s) what happens when fossil fuels are
burned? Circle all that apply.

    a. The amount of carbon in the   **c.** The amount of carbon in the
       atmosphere increases.   atmosphere decreases

    b. Nitrogen is changed to   **d.** Nitrogen is stored in
       a more usable form.   the ocean.

6. Draw lines to match the processes with the cycles of matter
they are part of. Processes can have more than 1 line drawn to them.

	Bacteria carry out fixation.
nitrogen cycle	Photosynthesis takes place.
carbon cycle	Decomposers break down dead organisms.
	Crops are fertilized by humans.
	Respiration takes place.

Lesson Roundup

A. Draw a line to match each term to its definition.

Evaporation	Water that falls from clouds to Earth's surface
Condensation	The process by which a liquid changes into a gas
Precipitation	The process by which a gas changes into a liquid

B. Draw a line to match each sphere to how it is affected by a volcanic eruption.

Atmosphere	New rock is produced and soil is enriched.
Geosphere	Plants and wildlife can be harmed by flowing lava.
Biosphere	Hot gases and ash are released into the air.

C. Choose the word that correctly completes each sentence.

directly	at an angle	even	uneven	warm	cold

Near the equator, the sun's rays strike Earth _____. These

areas are warmer. Wind is one effect of the _____ heating

of Earth's surface. _____ air near the equator rises in the

atmosphere. _____ air flows from the poles toward the equator.

D. Choose the word that correctly completes each sentence.

respiration	photosynthesis	decomposers	producers

The carbon cycle is an example of how Earth's spheres interact.

For example, carbon from the atmosphere is taken in by living things

and used for _____. _____ release carbon into

the soil when they break down dead organisms. The process of _____

releases carbon into the environment, including the atmosphere and hydrosphere.

What Is the Role of the Oceans in Earth's Systems?

Many scientists consider the ocean the last frontier on Earth because it is so vast, deep, and in some ways, difficult to explore.

By the end of this lesson . . .
you'll understand how the ocean affects Earth's systems.

Can You Explain It?

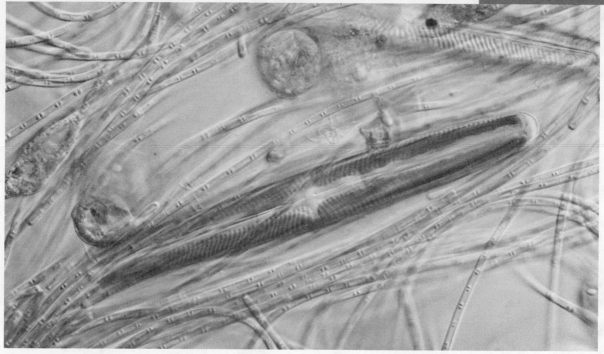

Did you know the world's oxygen is supplied mostly by tiny microscopic living things called *phytoplankton?* Phytoplankton also provides food for organisms throughout the ocean, from very small snails to very large baleen whales.

1. The organisms shown above live in the ocean. How do you think something so small could be the base of a food chain and the main provider of the world's oxygen?

_____

_____

_____

_____

_____

_____

_____

Tip

Learn more about the interactions of the atmosphere, hydrosphere, geosphere, and biosphere in How Do Earth's Systems Interact?

 EVIDENCE NOTEBOOK Look for this icon to help you gather evidence to answer the question above.

All about Oceans

Blue Planet

If you've ever looked at a globe, you have seen that much of Earth's surface is covered with water. In fact, water covers about 71% of the surface of Earth.

 Explore Online

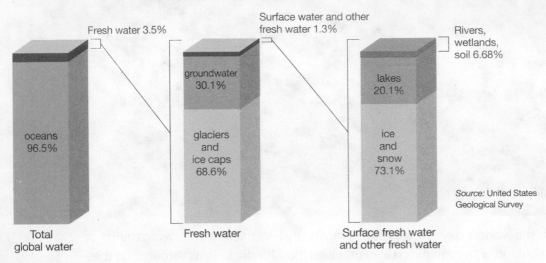

Distribution of Earth's Water

Fresh water 3.5%

Surface water and other fresh water 1.3%

Rivers, wetlands, soil 6.68%

oceans 96.5%

groundwater 30.1%

glaciers and ice caps 68.6%

lakes 20.1%

ice and snow 73.1%

Source: United States Geological Survey

Total global water

Fresh water

Surface fresh water and other fresh water

About 97% of Earth's surface water is salt water; just 3% is fresh water. Most salt water is found in the oceans. A small part of Earth's salt water is found in saltwater lakes. About 69% of Earth's fresh water is in icecaps and glaciers. Most of the remaining fresh water exists as groundwater, which we tap for use in homes and industry. Just over 1% of Earth's fresh water is surface water—what we see in lakes, rivers, and swamps.

Do the Math
Earth's Water

2. The grid to the right has 100 squares. Using the information above, fill in the grid with different colors to model the distribution of Earth's water. The whole grid represents 100%, so each square represents 1%. Use the space below to draw a key for your completed grid. The key should indicate which type of water or body of water each color represents in the grid. Note: You can split up squares to represent multiple things.

Salty, Saltier, Saltiest

You have learned that about 97% of the water on Earth is salty. The map below shows how saltiness, or salinity, can vary across the oceans.

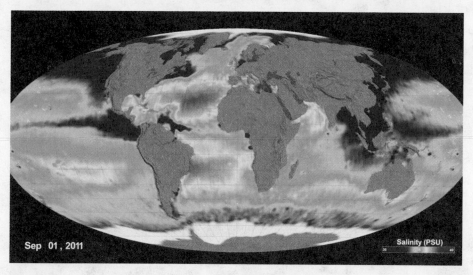

Sep 01, 2011

Salinity (PSU)

The Red Sea and Mediterranean Sea have higher salinity, on average, than other parts of the ocean. These variations are relatively small, but can affect the movement of ocean water in big ways!

3. Why do you think the salinity varies in different parts of the ocean? Think about how you might make a pot of soup less salty.

_____

_____

_____

_____

_____

HANDS-ON **Apply What You Know**

Salty Seas

4. Your teacher will provide you with a golf ball and two cups: one with fresh water and another with salt water. Place the golf ball in the fresh water and observe what happens. Then place the golf ball in the salt water and observe what happens. Compare your observations.

Think back to what you learned about salinity in the Mediterranean Sea and Red Sea . What is the relationship between the salinity of water and how easy it is for something to float or sink in water?

_____

_____

_____

Mixing Waters

▷ Explore Online

Anything that dives deep into the ocean, such as a submarine or a sperm whale, must be able to cope with a much darker, colder environment. It must also deal with tremendous pressure. All of the water above an organism or object presses down on it. In the deepest parts of the ocean, there are over 10 kilometers (6 miles) of water between the surface and ocean floor. That's deep enough to contain Mt. Everest.

Foam cups are 95% air. The air compresses as the cups are taken 1,500 m down into the ocean.

The oceans can be deep! The deeper you go, the greater the pressure is, due to the weight of the water above. Look at the chart. How much deeper is the habitat of the colossal squid than the habitat of deep sea sharks?

0 m	Sea level
40 m	casual dive limit
61 m	light fades
332 m	world scuba dive record
535 m	bottlenose dolphin feeding range
1,035 m	depth reached by U.S. submarines
1,800 m	habitat of deep sea sharks
2,197 m	habitat of the colossal squid
2,500 m	deepest recorded dive of a whale
3,790 m	average depth of the ocean
3,800 m	wreck of the Titanic
8,145 m	deepest known habitat for a fish
8,605 m	deepest part of the Atlantic Ocean
9,450 m	average altitude for an airliner (above the water)
10,683 m	deepest ocean drilling
10,911 m	deepest oceanic site: Mariana Trench

 5. Language SmArts Research and report on ocean submersibles. What do engineers need to consider when designing a submersible to withstand the pressures at the deepest parts of the oceans?

_____

_____

_____

What's at the Bottom of the Ocean?

The ocean isn't like a swimming pool, with edges that drop off steeply to a flat bottom. The ocean floor has many different features.

a. Around continents, there can be a relatively shallow area of ocean floor that extends many kilometers. This is called a **continental shelf.**

b. The **continental slope** is the steep area where the ocean rapidly gets deeper.

c. The **continental rise** is the lower part of the continental slope. It can reach 4,000 m (13,000 ft) below the ocean's surface.

d. In many parts of the ocean, there are long ridges of under sea mountains and volcanoes. These are called **mid-ocean ridges.**

e. The **abyssal plain** is the relatively flat, deep, vast area of the ocean floor.

f. A **trench** is a deep, valley-like part of the ocean floor, often near the edge of an island chain or continent.

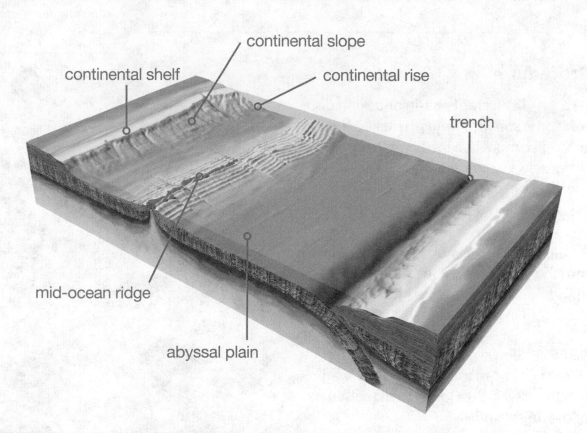

continental slope

continental shelf

continental rise

trench

mid-ocean ridge

abyssal plain

Putting It Together

6. Describe how the physical conditions around a submarine might change on a voyage from a coastal river to a deep-sea trench.

_____

_____

_____

_____

_____

How Do Oceans Shape Coastlines?

Objective

Collaborate to explore physical interactions between the hydrosphere and geosphere that occur at coastlines.

What question will you investigate to meet this objective?

_____

_____

Materials

- dishwashing basin or deep baking dish
- gloves
- soil
- sand
- water
- pitcher
- board

Procedure

STEP 1 In an empty basin or baking dish, mix some soil with water to make a thick, paste-like mud. Use the board to create a divider down the center of the basin. Pack the mud on one side. With the board in place, let the mud dry for a few days.

STEP 2 Once the mud has dried, pour sand into the empty side of the basin until it's about half as deep as the dried mud. Leave the board in place.

STEP 3 Slowly pour water from the pitcher on top of the sand until the water level is a few inches lower than the surface of the dried mud.

So far, excluding the board, what do you think your model is modeling?

_____

_____

_____

_____

STEP 4 Gently remove the board so the soil and sand do not mix much. Now have one person use the board to make waves. Press it straight down into the water at the side of the basin and then pull it back up. Do this repeatedly and observe what the waves do.

Record your observations.

Analyze Your Results

STEP 6 Describe how the waves affected the sand and soil.

_____

_____

_____

STEP 7 What characteristics or properties of sand allowed it to react to the movement of the waves as it did?

_____

_____

STEP 8 Compare your model and your results with those of other groups. How are they alike? How are they different?

_____

_____

Draw Conclusions

STEP 9 Why did you let the mud dry before you modeled the wave action?

_____

_____

STEP 10 Make a claim about how sandy beaches form. Cite evidence to support your claim.

_____

_____

_____

_____

Oceans Affect Landforms

Give and Take

Waves, currents, and other movements of ocean water can change coastlines by moving sand. A **coastline** is where land meets the ocean.

Ever-Changing Shore

7. Examine the images, and describe what you might see.

 Explore Online

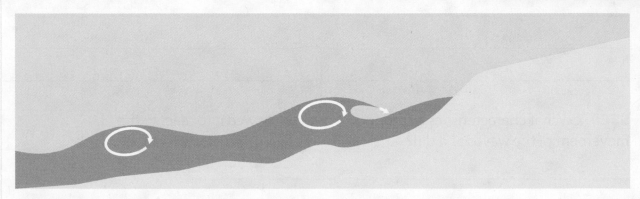

As waves roll in, they can carry sand and other material from deep water up onto shore.

_____

_____

_____

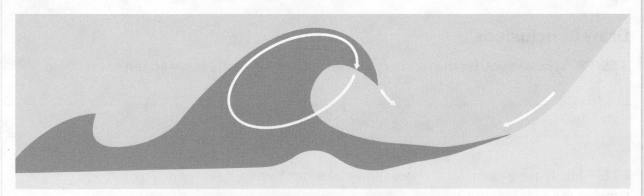

Waves can also transport sand from one part of the shore to another.

_____

_____

_____

Look at the images of changes to coastlines—one was gradual, and one was sudden.

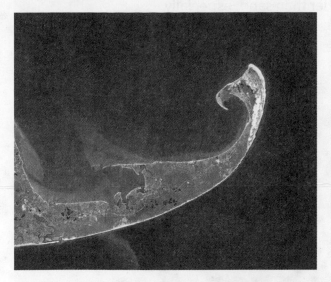

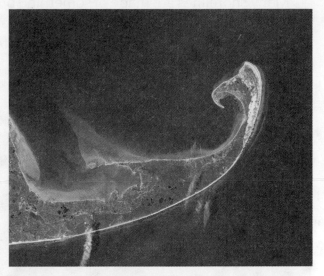

This is a satellite image of the southeast part of Cape Cod, a coastal area of Massachusetts. In the 1980s, the town of Chatham was protected by a long barrier beach called North Beach. To the south was Monomoy, a series of islands that are home to a National Wildlife Refuge.

Over the course of decades, severe winter storms broke through North Beach in several places. South Beach was disconnected from North Beach. Sand from the new inlet washed in and connected South Beach to the mainland. The islands of Monomoy were also reshaped.

2006

2011

This satellite image shows a beach in Sendai, Japan.

This satellite image shows the same beach after a massive earthquake sent devastating tsunami waves onto Sendai's shore.

 8. Language SmArts Describe how the ocean can reshape coastlines in ways that are both gradual and sudden.

_____

_____

_____

Rocky Shores

Many shorelines are made of something other than sand, especially where there is a steep drop-off. These coasts are often made of rock. But even rock can be worn down by wind and water over time.

▶ Explore Online

On the coast of Ireland are the Cliffs of Moher. The cliffs are made of different layers of rock that are hundreds of millions of years old. The layers are made of compacted sand, silt, and mud that used to be under water. Rain, waves, and wind have weathered and eroded the cliffs over time, exposing how the layers of rock formed some 300 million years ago.

9. Complete each sentence by selecting the correct word.

cliffs	**wind**	**silt**	**rain**
waves	**layers**	**fossils**	**weathering**

The Cliffs of Moher are an example of how _____ can shape

coastal rock formations. Both _____ and _____

have weathered the cliffs with water. _____ has also played a role

in shaping the cliffs over time.

 EVIDENCE NOTEBOOK Record evidence of how the ocean has reshaped cliffs over time.

Beach Rescue

Coastal erosion can change shores in ways that affect people. For example, a town whose beach attracts summer tourists may not have any business if the beach is washed away. And millions of people live on or near the shore, meaning their lives depend on the coastline not changing too much. Explore the images to see what humans and other organisms can do to minimize coastal change.

Sand can be brought in from elsewhere if a popular beach is heavily eroded. The new sand may have been dredged from the nearby ocean floor, or it may have been trucked in from far away. This can be an expensive operation.

Seawalls are built to prevent beach sand from being washed away by waves or heavy storms. Preventing erosion is often cheaper than fixing it after the damage already has been done.

Estuaries, such as this mangrove forest, are coastal ecosystems that serve as buffers between land and sea. Plants that grow in this habitat—and the muddy sediment they take root in—can absorb some of the force of coastal storms and high tides.

Putting It Together

10. A tropical sandy beach is 200 meters long but just 30 meters wide at high tide. Behind it is a row of hotels that support the local economy. At both ends of the beach are mangrove forests. A hotel owner wants to remove the mangroves to build new hotels. How will the removal of trees affect the beach and the economy? Explain.

_____

_____

_____

Oceans Affect Climate

Heater and Cooler

You have probably heard of or perhaps experienced the ocean's surface currents. There are also currents that move below the surface.

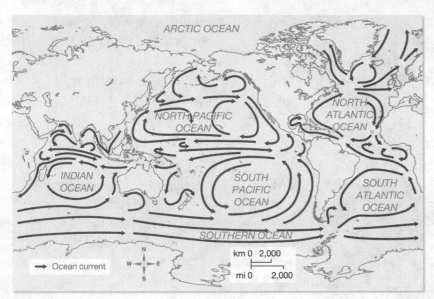

This map shows the major surface currents. These are driven mainly by winds.

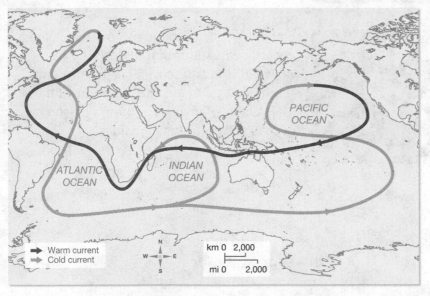

The ocean also has a pattern of slower currents that move surface water beginning in the cold North Atlantic to warmer areas near the equator. The cold water sinks deep down, and slowly warms and rises back to the surface, bringing nutrients up with it. Scientists call this global current "the global ocean conveyor belt."

The conveyor belt current transports huge amounts of seawater, which means thermal energy, nutrients, and even organisms are transported as well. Warm surface currents transfer energy as heat into the atmosphere, which helps moderate the climate in areas that would otherwise be much colder. If the conveyor belt were to stop, the effects on climate and ocean food chains could be catastrophic.

Greenland

equator

To understand how the global ocean conveyor belt works, it helps to see it from the side. In the very cold waters of the North Atlantic Ocean, water loses energy to the frigid air and floating masses of ice at the surface. Water becomes heaviest at temperatures just above freezing. Salt water freezes, but the salt does not; it remains in the surrounding liquid ocean water. The heavier, saltier water sinks down, as shown here by the green arrows. Warm water from the tropics flows to the north to replace the water that sinks from the surface.

11. Choose the correct words to complete the sentences.

winds	currents	warmer	less salty	saltier	colder

The global ocean conveyor belt is a pattern of _____

that helps distribute energy and nutrients throughout the ocean.

In the North Atlantic part of the conveyor belt, surface water sinks

down toward the ocean floor after becoming _____ and

_____. _____ water from the tropics flows

to the north to replace what sank from the surface.

 EVIDENCE NOTEBOOK How does the ocean affect the atmosphere and hydrosphere? Record your evidence in your Evidence Notebook.

El Niño and La Niña

The ocean has a huge impact on climate due to its transport of thermal energy and its role in the water cycle. Climates and weather patterns around the planet can change if conditions in the ocean change, even if the change occurs in just one part of the ocean.

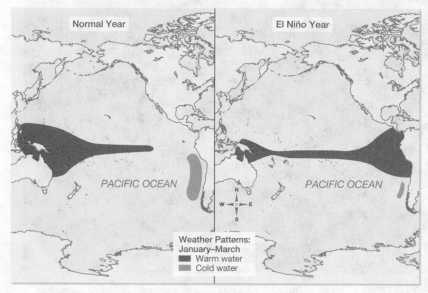

In a typical year, the wind over the central Pacific Ocean blows from east to west. In an El Niño year, the ocean surface temperature in the tropical Pacific is unusually warm. The east-to-west trade winds weaken, altering ocean currents and atmospheric conditions across the central Pacific. Rain clouds that normally form in the western Pacific form in the east instead. The wind may even turn around and blow from west to east.

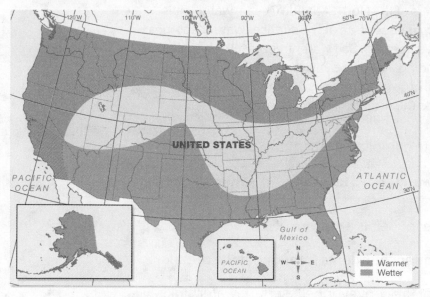

In the United States, an El Niño event usually means warmer, drier winter weather in the northern half of the continental United States and wetter, cooler winter weather in the southern half.

12. How would you prepare for winter during an El Niño year?

_____

_____

_____

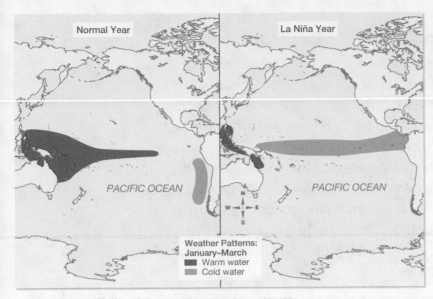

Some years feature an El Niño event, while others experience a La Niña event. La Niña is caused by unusually cool sea surface temperatures in the central Pacific. Many of its effects are the opposite of El Niño's effects.

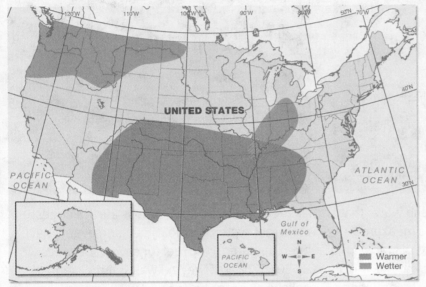

La Niña's effect on winter weather in the United States is the opposite of El Niño's. The northern half is colder and wetter than usual, which may mean more snow and greater risk of flooding in the spring. The southern half is warmer and drier than usual, which in southern states may cause droughts or make them worse.

13. Language SmArts Compare and contrast an El Niño event with a typical year. Be sure to discuss conditions in the central Pacific that cause an El Niño and the results that are likely to affect the continental United States.

_____

_____

_____

_____

_____

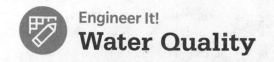

Engineer It!
Water Quality

The temperature increase at the surface of the Pacific Ocean is just a few degrees during an El Niño event. Small changes in ocean water can affect all organisms in an ocean food chain. This is why marine scientists measure the changes to seawater all over the planet.

Climate change is causing the temperature of the ocean to rise in many locations. Many corals are extremely sensitive to temperature changes. If the temperature of the ocean water increases by just a few degrees, the corals turn white, or look bleached. Tiny algae that live inside the corals are expelled, making corals look white. If the bleaching event lasts long enough, the corals can die.

Temperature is one property of ocean water that scientists test. Some scientists also measure other important properties: salinity, pH (acidity), dissolved oxygen levels, and how clear the water is. These properties can be affected by pollution.

Australia's Great Barrier Reef is Earth's largest coral reef system. Major bleaching events have been damaging the reef for several decades. By 2016, 22% of the reef was dead. Scientists believe climate change and El Niño were the cause.

Putting It Together

14. How might a tropical Pacific island that is ringed by coral reef and its inhabitants be affected by El Niño and climate change?

_____

_____

_____

_____

_____

_____

Oceans Affect Ecosystems

Diversity of the Deep

The ocean includes the sunlit shallows off a sandy beach and the cold, pitch-black depths of the Marianas Trench. The wide range of conditions in the ocean means there's also great diversity of habitats. Temperature, depth, pressure, the availability of light, and other factors help define these habitats, or zones, of the ocean.

In areas where the ocean floor is not very deep, plants and plant-like algae, which you may know as seaweed, can receive sunlight and photosynthesize—use sunlight to make food. The algae that live inside corals also use sunlight to make food.

Far from shore, in deep water, the only photosynthetic organisms are the phytoplankton that float in the water near the surface. The water is too deep for photosynthetic corals and seaweed. Some organisms don't leave the upper levels of the ocean, while others live in the deepest, darkest depths despite the absence of sunlight and the tremendous pressure.

 EVIDENCE NOTEBOOK Photosynthetic organisms usually make up the lowest levels of food chains. What do you think this means about ocean food chains? Record your ideas in your Evidence Notebook.

Blooming

Phytoplankton can thrive in the open ocean zone if conditions are right. Nutrients are a key ingredient in causing a phytoplankton "bloom"—a sudden explosion of their population. Upwelling can bring nutrient-rich water from the deep sea up to the sunlit areas where phytoplankton can use them. When a bloom occurs, huge swaths of sea can turn green with phytoplankton.

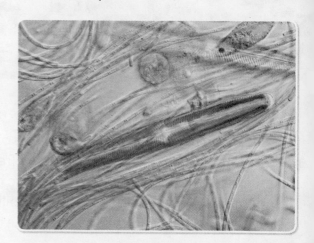

HANDS-ON Apply What You Know

Losing Light

15. With a partner and guidance from your teacher, complete this activity to see how light is filtered out by water the deeper you go.

Procedure

a. Add five drops of blue food coloring to a pitcher of water, and mix.

b. Pour some of the water into a small beaker or glass.

c. One of you should hold the pitcher of blue water about 4 feet off the ground. The other student should kneel or duck below, and look straight up through the blue water inside the pitcher while holding the flashlight above the pitcher and aiming the light directly down. Think of what you see as a model of sunlight penetrating deep, clear ocean water.

d. Repeat b, this time using the small beaker or glass of blue water. This time you are modeling sunlight in a shallow habitat.

16. Choose the correct words to complete the sentences.

phytoplankton	fish	sunlight	pressure

Plants, algae, and _____ are limited to ocean zones

that are within the first few hundred meters of depth. This is because

_____ cannot penetrate beyond that depth. But there

are organisms that live in the deepest parts of the ocean, despite the

darkness and extreme _____.

The Ins, Outs, Ups, and Downs of Life on the Shoreline

Life changes with the tides in the waters of the ocean's intertidal zone.

Tidal Life

 Explore Online

In intertidal zones, organisms are adapted to rapidly changing conditions. At high tide there's plenty of water to provide food and oxygen. Crabs emerge, and fish that went out with the tide can come back looking for food.

The tidal pool stays wet even when the tide is low or completely out, thanks to the pool-like shape of the shore. Sea stars hunt for mussels, snails feed on algae, and crabs are busy looking for food or mates.

17. Circle all the issues that organisms of the intertidal zone have to cope with at low tide.

a. Some organisms will be more exposed to predators.

b. Organisms that get oxygen from water will have to survive without it for several hours.

c. Organisms that live in fresh water have to live in salt water.

d. Organisms will have to adjust to changes in temperature.

e. The sunlight and the air causes some organisms to become warm and dry.

18. Language SmArts The crab stays in the intertidal zone at high tide and low tide. Research how its behavior changes from one tide to the next. What's the connection between the crab's changing behavior and its changing environment?

_____

_____

_____

_____

Life Offshore

In the open ocean, much of the productivity occurs in the upper levels where sunlight can be used by phytoplankton to produce food. The phytoplankton are the first link in a food chain.

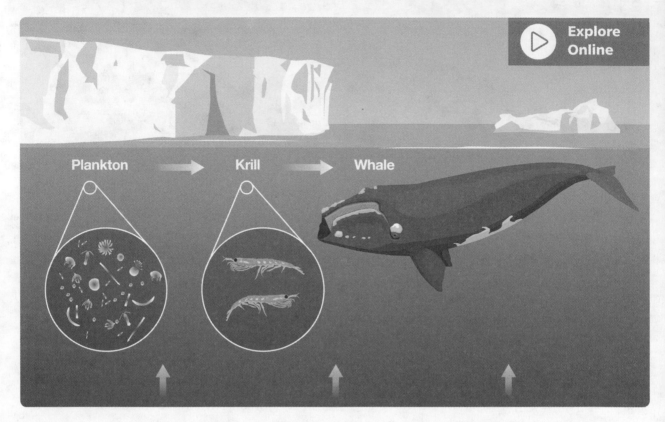

In the summer, Antarctica receives a lot of sunlight, which is needed for photosynthesis. Remember the giant ocean conveyor belt? Around Antarctica, the conveyor belt causes upwelling—like an upside-down waterfall that carries water from the deep ocean up to the surface. This upwelling is rich with nutrients that, when combined with sunlight, cause phytoplankton populations to grow rapidly. A shrimplike animal called krill then eats the phytoplankton. Krill are food for many different animals in the Southern Ocean around Antarctica, from penguins to southern right whales.

Putting It Together

19. Compare and contrast how organisms in the open ocean and intertidal zone live. Discuss how both are affected by tides and the types of organisms that live in them.

_____

_____

_____

_____

Discover More

Check out this path . . . or go online to choose one of these other paths.

People in Science & Engineering

- **The Gulf Stream**
- **Harnessing Wave Energy**

Warren Washington and David Sandwell

► Explore Online

There are many science careers that involve studying the ocean. Dr. Warren Washington is a senior scientist at the National Center for Atmospheric Research. He has been working on climate models since the 1960s, including models that predict how conditions in the ocean affect the atmosphere.

Dr. Washington and other climate scientists were awarded a Nobel Prize in 2007 for their work in analyzing and modeling climate change. Washington has advised five U.S. presidents and published more than 150 papers on climate science topics. In 2010, he was awarded the National Medal of Science. He earned his Ph.D. in meteorology, the study of weather patterns.

Climate models incorporate all the interconnected parts and systems—hydrosphere, geosphere, atmosphere, and biosphere—that influence climate. They can be used to analyze past, present, and future. Currently, many climate models are being developed to help us understand climate change and what can be done to slow or halt it.

Dr. David Sandwell is a geologist at the Scripps Institute of Oceanography of the University of California. He specializes in studies of the Earth's crust, including mid-ocean ridges and other formations on the ocean floor.

Dr. Sandwell's research embraces technology, including satellites that analyze the ocean surface and sonar devices that can map the ocean floor. He teaches several courses—including one called The Physics of Surfing—while advising Ph.D. students. He has published over 160 scientific papers. He earned his Ph.D. in geophysics, the study of Earth's physical properties and processes.

Sonar is a technology that uses sound waves sent down into the ocean to create visuals of the ocean floor and other objects. Dr. Sandwell has worked on using satellite technology to map the ocean floor.

20. In college, both Dr. Washington and Dr. Sandwell majored in physics, the study of properties of matter and energy. How do you think this helped them pursue their careers, and what does physics have to do with the ocean?

_____

_____

_____

_____

_____

Lesson Check

Name _____

Can You Explain It?

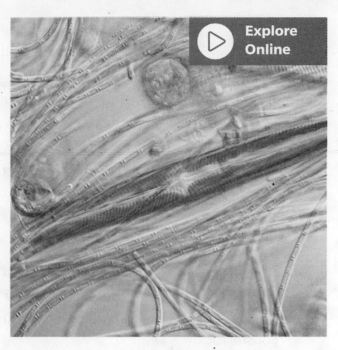

Explore Online

1. Now that you've learned more about how the oceans affect the rest of Earth's spheres, explain how the microscopic phytoplankton shown here can have a major role in the biosphere. In your answer, be sure to do the following:

- Discuss the role of photosynthetic organisms in marine food chains.

- Identify at least two different habitats or ocean zones where phytoplankton live.

- Describe the role of currents and other physical processes and properties of ocean water that affect the biosphere.

EVIDENCE NOTEBOOK Use the information you've collected in your Evidence Notebook to help you cover each point.

_____

_____

_____

_____

_____

_____

_____

_____

Checkpoints

2. Which of the following features of the ocean floor is similar to a rift valley, where Earth's crust is split and the two sides are moving apart?

   a. mid-ocean ridge   **c.** trench

   b. volcanic island   **d.** canyon

3. Match the events or processes to their descriptions.

| erosion | tsunami | weathering | breakwaters and seawalls |

_____ a massive wave that causes severe erosion and other damage on coastlines, usually following an earthquake

_____ waves striking a rocky outcropping that extends from the seashore, slowly breaking down the rock into smaller pieces

_____ a winter storm that is most severe at high tide sends waves over a barrier beach, creating a new inlet to a small bay

_____ walls constructed by humans to prevent erosion and other wave-related damage on the shoreline

4. Look at the photo. Why do you think sand is being deposited at this beach?

a. Erosion has removed sand from the beach. Danger from coastal storms is a problem.

b. Sand is being moved to replace weathering of coastal rock.

c. Too many people are building sandcastles, which loosens the sand and causes erosion.

d. Geologists predict sand will erode from this beach and drift to another beach nearby.

5. Read the following weather forecast:

In Southern California this winter, expect heavy rainfall and cooler temperatures and maybe a cyclone or two, depending on just how unusually warm the water gets in the central Pacific. This event could be worse than the last one.

What is being described?

a. typical stormy winter weather for the region

b. La Niña event

c. climate change

d. El Niño event

6. Which of the following are features of the ocean conveyor belt? Circle all that apply.

a. high salinity and low temperature of surface water near the North Pole

b. Gulf Stream current carrying cold water from Florida up through and across the North Atlantic Ocean toward Europe

c. upwelling bringing nutrients from the deep sea up toward the surface near landmasses such as Antarctica

d. undersea volcanic activity heating large amounts of ocean water, causing it to rise to the surface

Lesson Roundup

A. Label each type of water from 1 to 5 in terms of greatest percentage of Earth's water (1 is highest).

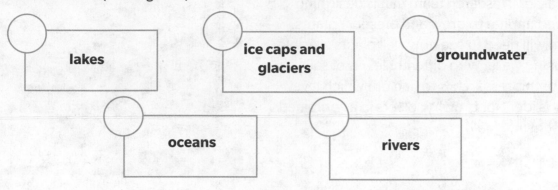

lakes

ice caps and glaciers

groundwater

oceans

rivers

B. Which of the following are ways to protect beaches from tidal waves? Circle all that apply.

a. Replenish beaches with sand to protect against higher and larger waves.

b. Build seawalls or breakwaters to minimize erosion.

c. Build new houses and hotels on the shore.

d. Close hiking trails on cliffs that might have loose or cracked rocks.

C. Choose the correct words to complete each sentence.

open ocean	mid-ocean ridge	intertidal zone
phytoplankton	high tide	trench

At Yellowtail Point, the _____ begins at the beach and extends

out about 50 meters, where the low tide meets a clump of kelp and boulders.

Large fish move in during _____ to feed on crabs and other

animals that emerge from the rocks and sand, then the fish head back out to

the _____ at low tide. The water is often green near Yellowtail

Point because upwelling causes blooms of _____, thanks to the

nutrients being brought up from the ocean floor.

ENGINEER IT!
Saltwater Plants

You are part of a research team that is designing a contained habitat to grow and preserve plants. Your team will need to see how well plants are able to grow using water with different levels of salinity. The goal of this research is to find out which level of salinity is ideal for growing plants in a contained environment.

FIND A PROBLEM: What problem do you need to solve? Before beginning, look at the checklist at the end of this project to be sure you are meeting all the requirements.

_____

_____

RESEARCH: Find the range of salinity in which plants can grow and measure the salinity of each water sample you plan to use for watering the plants during your test. Record the data for each type of water.

_____

_____

BRAINSTORM: Brainstorm three or more ideas with your team to solve the problem. Keep in mind the criteria and constraints.

_____

_____

_____

Criteria	Constraints
☐ Plant must survive.	☐ Plants must be grown indoors.
☐ The environment must be conducive for growing plants.	☐ Plants will be grown in pots or containers.
☐ There must be a large enough difference in the salinity levels of the water.	☐ Plants will be watered manually, 2–3 times per day.

MAKE A PLAN: Make a plan by considering the questions below. Answer the questions and make a list of needed materials and why you need them.

1. What supplies will you need to carry out this research and why?

2. Describe your plant-growing environment in terms of sun exposure, controlled temperature, and soil.

_____

_____

_____

DESIGN: Design the contained habitat for growing the plants. Include the structure of the environment, the placement/location of the plants in relation to the sun, and how far apart the plants will be situated from each other.

EVALUATE AND REDESIGN: Did you meet the criteria and constraints? What are some ways you can improve the experiment?

_____

_____

_____

COMMUNICATE: Present your design to the class using multimedia.

✓ Checklist

Review your project and check off each completed item.

_____ Includes a list of what conditions are ideal for growing plants.

_____ Includes the levels of salinity in each sample of water.

_____ Includes a list of the supplies needed for carrying out the research.

_____ Includes a design of the contained habitat.

_____ Includes a list of potential problems with solutions.

Unit Review

1. What kind of water is depicted in the solid in the image?

   a. salt water

   b. water vapor

   c. groundwater

   d. fresh water

2. Compare the processes of weathering and erosion by writing the phrases into the Venn diagram.

   > **breaking down rocks**
   >
   > **moving sediment one place to another**
   >
   > **cause change to geosphere**
   >
   > **caused by water flow**

Weathering	Both	Erosion

3. Aaron is researching characteristics of the ocean. Which statement about oceans is true?

   a. People float more easily in saltier water.

   b. The ocean is cooler toward the surface.

   c. Most human activity on the ocean is done out at sea.

   d. Sunlight becomes brighter as the ocean gets deeper.

4. Which natural process was responsible for the rocky coastline in the image?

   a. weathering

   b. precipitation

   c. melting

   d. sedimentation

5. Circle the word that correctly completes the sentence. The troposphere/stratosphere/mesosphere is the layer of the atmosphere we live in.

6. Which object in the image is responsible for condensation?

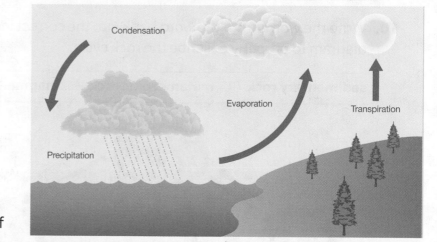

   a. sun

   b. ocean

   c. green land

   d. dark cloud

   e. white cloud

7. Which of the following is true of El Niño and La Niña events?

   a. They both cause cooling in the Atlantic Ocean.

   b. They both cause prolonged drought in North America.

   c. They both relate to temperature changes in the Pacific Ocean.

   d. They both cause predictable shifts in seasonal patterns of temperature and precipitation.

8. What effect does wind have on the water cycle, over the oceans?

    a. It increases evaporation.

    b. It decreases evaporation.

    c. It slows condensation.

    d. It speeds up precipitation.

9. Sort the characteristics by the Earth spheres they describe.

made up of air	contains all solid land	extends to Earth's core
the most massive system	made up of water	overlaps with other spheres
	covers about 75% of Earth's surface	

Atmosphere	Geosphere	Hydrosphere

10. Write the words from the word bank into the correct location on the diagram to properly describe the rock cycle.

| sedimentary rock | metamorphic rock | magma | sediments |

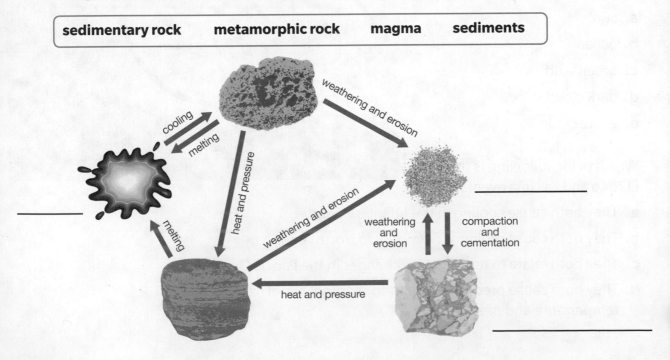

442

Earth and Human Activities

Explore Online

Unit Project: My Environmental Impact
What is the total amount of recyclable material you will use in your life? You will conduct an investigation with your team. Ask your teacher for details.

How has human activity impacted the land in this picture?

UNIT 7

At a Glance

Vocabulary Game: Picture It

Materials
- Kitchen timer or online computer timer
- Sketch pad

How to Play
1. Take turns to play.

2. To take a turn, choose a word from the Word Box. Do not tell the word to the other players.

3. Set the timer for 1 minute.

4. Draw pictures on the sketch pad to give clues about the word. Draw only pictures and numbers. Do not use words.

5. The first player to guess the word gets 1 point. If that player can use the word in a sentence, he or she gets 1 more point. Then that player gets a turn to choose a word.

6. The first player to score 5 points wins.

recycle

population

Unit Vocabulary

biodegradable: Able to be decomposed by living organisms.

population: All the organisms of the same kind that live together in a given area.

conserve: To preserve and protect an ecosystem or a resource.

recycle: To use the materials in old things to make new things.

decompose: Breaking down dead organisms and animal wastes into simpler substances to get energy.

reduce: To use less of something.

natural resource: Anything from nature that people can use.

reuse: To use something again.

pollution: Any waste product or contamination that harms or dirties an ecosystem and harms organisms.

How Does Resource Use Affect Earth?

When people move into cities, those cities grow and spread out.
How does this growth affect the land and other resources?

By the end of this lesson . . .
you'll be able to recognize and explain how people affect Earth's resources.

Can You Explain It?

 Explore Online

In 1900, Las Vegas was a tiny town in the desert of Nevada with only 22 residents. By 1930, about 5,000 people lived there. Today, the population of Las Vegas is around 2 million. Las Vegas is in the desert, and city planners are trying to find ways to protect water supplies and other resources for the future.

1972

1990

2010

This satellite image shows Las Vegas from the air in 1972. The red areas represent actual green space, such as, golf courses and city parks.

Over time, as people move into an area, they change the landscape. They build roads and houses.

Small towns can become cities. Eventually, the landscape no longer looks the way it once did.

1. Las Vegas is an example of a city, in which the population has has increased over time. What are some ways that growing populations affect Earth's resources?

_____

_____

_____

_____

_____

_____

_____

_____

Tip

Learn more about Earth's systems and the resources they hold in How Do Earth's Systems Interact? and What Is the Role of Water in Earth's Systems?

 EVIDENCE NOTEBOOK Look for this icon to help you gather evidence to answer the question above.

Earth's Resources

Renewable versus Nonrenewable

A **natural resource** is anything from nature that people can use. It can be renewable or nonrenewable. *Renewable resources* are replaced by natural processes in a fairly short time, and are clean. *Nonrenewable resources* are used up faster than they can be replaced, and cause pollution. It's important to **conserve** resources to preserve and protect an ecosystem or resource.

Classifying Resources

2. Read about each resource below, and then draw a circle around the renewable resources and a square around the nonrenewable resources.

a. **Natural gas** is a fossil fuel used to generate electricity. We can conserve it by using less natural gas and more renewable resources.

b. **Water** is necessary for all forms of life to survive on Earth. Hydroelectric energy stations use flowing water to generate electricity.

c. **Sunlight,** or solar energy, warms Earth's surface. People use solar energy to generate electricity, heat water, and even cook food.

d. **Minerals** are used to make metals, jewelry, and other products. The supply is dropping rapidly as demand increases. They can take up to millions of years to form.

e. **Soil** is used by humans for growing food, and it provides a habitat for many living things. It can take up to millions of years to form.

f. **Oil** is a fossil fuel used to generate electricity, and is also used as fuel for vehicles. We can conserve oil by limiting our use of it.

g. **Wind** is the movement of air. Wind can make huge wind turbines turn, which generates electricity. Wind energy is clean and affordable.

h. **Trees** are used to build homes, furniture, and other products. People can replant trees in areas where trees have been removed.

I. **Coal** is a fossil fuel that forms underground from the remains of plants that lived long ago. People burn coal for heat and to generate electricity. It takes millions of years to form.

Human Activities and Earth's Systems

As you have learned, Earth is made up of systems that interact together. The geosphere is Earth's dirt, rocks, and landforms. The hydrosphere is Earth's water systems. The atmosphere is Earth's air and other gases. The biosphere is where Earth's plants and animals live. Read about how each system is affected by some human activities below.

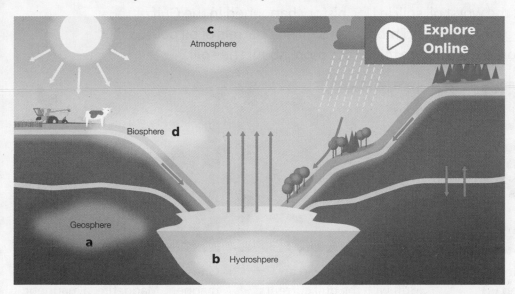

a. Geosphere Littering causes pollution of the geosphere and, potentially, all of Earth's systems. **Pollution** is any waste product or contamination that harms an ecosystem.

b. Hydrosphere Overfishing disrupts the balance of wildlife within a body of water. This can lead to an entire food chain being affected.

c. Atmosphere Deforestation causes negative impacts on the the atmosphere, because trees provide oxygen, and remove carbon from the air. Deforestation also affects the other spheres.

d. Biosphere Converting forests into agricultural land can result in loss of habitat. Many different species can be lost during this conversion.

3. Research additional human activities that affect each sphere. Record your findings below.

_____

_____

_____

4. José is organizing a park cleanup program. Which of Earth's spheres can be helped by José's cleanup program?

_____

_____

Oil Spills

▷ Explore Online

Pools of oil collect deep underground between layers of rock. Getting the oil out is not easy. Powerful drills bore into the rock layers to remove it. In April 2010, the worst oil spill in U.S. history happened in the Gulf of Mexico. An oil rig exploded, and more than 3 million barrels of oil poured into the gulf. Look at each image to find out more about the spill.

The Deepwater Horizon oil spill was located 68 kilometers off the coast of Louisiana, in the Gulf of Mexico.

Oil began to spread and drift with the gulf currents. Scientists say the oil slick at the surface reached a length of 35 kilometers.

One way to clean up oil spills uses magnets. Magnetite, a magnetic mineral, is sprinkled on the loose oil. Then a magnet pulls the magnetized oil out of the water.

5. Research different methods that have been used to clean oil spills. Work as a team to design a way to clean up an oil spill. On a separate sheet of paper, draw your technology, give it a name, and label its parts. Share your design with your classmates. Describe your technology. How will it clean up oil spills?

_____

_____

_____

Make sure your design meets the following criteria and constraints.

Criteria	Constraints
☐ Your design must clean up oil spills without adding more pollutants to the environment.	☐ You will have to complete your design within the alloted time given by your teacher.
☐ Your design must be based on existing technology and scientifically valid ideas.	

Protecting Our Earth Research Project

Create a brochure to show how one of Earth's systems is affected by human activities.

A brochure is an eye-catching, folded piece of paper that provides useful facts about a particular topic. Decide which of Earth's systems you are going to focus on. Collect and record information from personal experiences, books, and online research, then paraphrase that information. Also provide one or more solutions for the issues involving your system. Be sure to cite your references. Present your brochure to the rest of the class.

Include the following details: a title, current issues involving the sphere, what is being done to resolve the issues, renewable and nonrenewable resources affected, and a list of information sources used.

6. What new information did you learn in creating your brochure?

_____

_____

 EVIDENCE NOTEBOOK Gather evidence of how the Deepwater Horizon oil spill affected wildlife populations in the Gulf of Mexico. Write your findings in your Evidence Notebook.

 Language SmArts
Main Idea and Details

7. Write the correct answer for each sentence on the line.

atmosphere	hydrosphere	magnetic
geosphere	nonrenewable	renewable

Oil is a _____ resource. To remove the

oil, drills bore into the _____. During the

Deepwater Horizon oil spill, barrels of oil poured into the

_____. Making oil _____

is one possible method for cleaning up oil spills.

Tip

The English Language Arts Handbook can provide help with understanding how to identify the main idea and details.

Earth and Human Activity

Problems and Solutions

A **population** is all the organisms of the same kind that live together in a given area. Scientists who study human population growth have shown that the number of humans on Earth has been increasing.

In modern times, advancements in medicine and technology make it possible for humans to live longer, so even more people inhabit Earth. Study the graph below showing how the human population has grown over time.

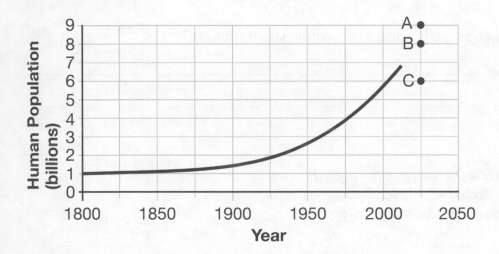

8. Look at the graph. What do you think the human population will be in the year 2025?

   a. 9 billion   **b.** 8 billion   **c.** 6 billion

9. How do you think human population growth affects Earth?

_____

_____

_____

10. Why do you think the population began to grow rapidly in the 1900s?

_____

_____

_____

Growing, Growing . . .

What happens as the number of people on Earth increases? Examine the graphs below to learn more about how population growth and the production of municipal solid waste (MSW) are related. MSW is waste produced by the public. Look for a trend—a general way something changes—in the information shown on the graphs.

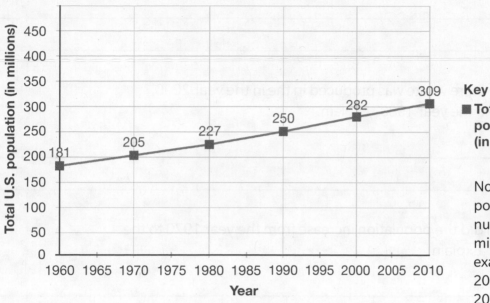

Key

■ Total U.S. population (in millions)

Note: In the population graph, the numbers represent millions of people. For example, the value 205 is equivalent to 205,000,000 people.

11. How has the human population changed over time?

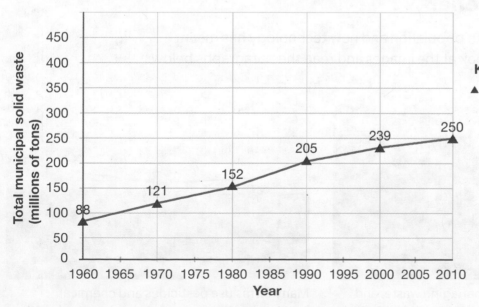

Key

▲ Total MSW (millions of tons)

Note: In the municipal solid waste graph, the numbers represent millions of tons of municipal solid waste. For example, the value 121 is equivalent to 121,000,000 tons of municipal solid waste.

12. How has the amount of MSW changed over time?

Do the Math

Calculate Energy Units

Read and answer the questions below. Refer to the graphs on page 453.

13. What trends do you notice in the MSW graph? What trends do you notice in the population graph?

_____

_____

14. How much more waste was produced in the in the year 2000, compared to the year 1980? Explain.

_____

_____

15. How much did the population increase from the year 1970 to the year 2010? Explain.

_____

_____

What's Being Done?

An increase in human population and new technology has meant new issues for Earth. Look at the images and read the paragraphs below each one to learn more.

Maintaining structures, managing waste, and providing enough energy are challenges facing expanding cities. Many are trying to solve these problems with recycling programs, community farm projects, and transportation systems.

Many farms use pesticides and chemical fertilizers to boost crop production. But health concerns connected to these substances have led some farmers to using methods that help protect the soil, water, crops, and people.

Dams redirect the flow of rivers and streams, destroy habitats, and disrupt the life cycle of many animals. Many dams are being removed in an effort to restore habitats and other resources.

Ocean debris is composed mostly of plastic—and it is accumulating. Many places no longer allow the use of plastic bags, and groups around the world meet regularly to clean up coastlines.

More people means more vehicles on the roads. Cars that run on fossil fuels release pollutants into the air. The auto industry has helped address this problem with hybrid and electric cars.

not to scale

Space exploration and satellite technology have resulted in much space debris. Scientists are working on a plan to fire beams of gas at the space debris, causing it to fall to Earth and burn up.

16. Complete the table below showing the problems connected to human population growth and some of the solutions to those problems.

Problem	Solution
dam	removal and restoration of habitats
trash in the ocean	ban the use of plastic bags; join beach cleanup groups

The Amazon

The Amazon rain forest covers 5,500,000 square kilometers and over 40% of the country of Brazil. Millions of species live there. Rain forests also help clean the air and play a key role in the water cycle. Large parts of the forest have been cut down for farming and development. Look at the pictures to see how deforestation has changed the rain forest.

Explore Online

1976

1994

2012

17. How did the rain forest change over time? How might these changes affect the rest of the biosphere and other Earth systems?

_____

_____

_____

Engineer It!

Space Junk

Scientists estimate that 500,000 pieces of space debris are orbiting Earth. These objects include old satellites, parts of satellites, and meteoroids. The entire collection of all these objects is referred to as "space junk." Many solutions are being developed to remove this debris. Look at the images to learn more about some of these solutions.

Of special interest to the space cleanup solutions are the numerous cube satellites orbiting Earth. These 10–centimeter–square satellites are used to provide weather data, space images, and other research information. Many cube satellites are no longer in use. How can we safely get rid of them?

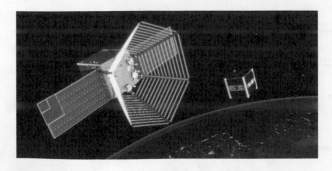

One solution is to use a satellite with a large net to capture the cube satellites. After capture, both satellites would descend into Earth's atmosphere. There, they would burn up.

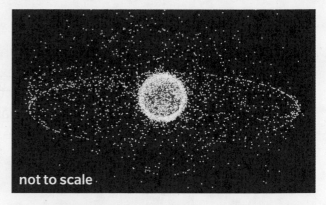

not to scale

The most practical solution seems to be using a satellite that acts as a slingshot. It captures the space debris, flings it down to Earth's atmosphere to burn up, and then uses energy from the flinging motion to accelerate toward the next piece. This helps save fuel, which is one of the biggest challenges in designing a space vehicle to collect the debris.

The 500,000 pieces of "space junk" orbiting Earth are the size of a marble or larger. Twenty thousand of those pieces are the size of softballs or larger. Imagine the danger these particles pose to space stations, astronauts, and probes.

 HANDS-ON Apply What You Know

Cleaning Up Space Debris

In a group, research pictures of space debris. Draw a diagram of an invention that could clean up the debris, and explain how the invention works. Make sure to submit your diagram and explanation to your teacher.

Make sure your design meets the following criteria and constraints:

Criteria	Constraints
☐ Your group's invention must use materials that can withstand the elements of space. ☐ You must be able to explain how your invention will work remotely by computer control.	☐ You will have to complete your design within the allotted time given by your teacher.

18. What was the most difficult part of your task? What was the easiest part?

_____

_____

_____

Too Many Layers

Look at the images of each example showing wasteful packaging. Wasteful packaging describes unnecessary, extra packaging that does not make a product better. Many products we buy include a lot of unnecessary packaging. Decreasing this wasteful packaging can decrease the total amount of generated waste.

Overpackaging

19. Look through each of the images showing examples of wasteful packaging, then answer the questions.

What product is shown? How could the packaging of this product be reduced?

_____

_____

_____

_____

What product is shown? How could the packaging of this product be reduced?

_____

_____

_____

_____

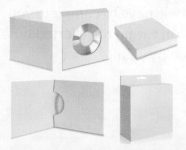

What product is shown? How could the packaging of this product be reduced?

_____

_____

_____

_____

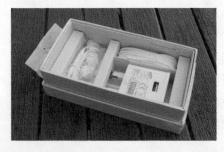

What product is shown? How could the packaging of this product be reduced?

_____

_____

_____

_____

20. Fill out a Claims and Evidence Chart. Make a claim about a product you feel is overpackaged. If you need to, conduct research online or at the library. Use three facts you learned from your research to provide evidence for your claim.

Claim	Evidence

Present your claim to your classmates. Debate your claim if necessary.

21. How can we reduce the amount of overpackaging in items?

_____

_____

22. Language SmArts How would you paraphrase the information you learned here about overpackaging?

_____

_____

_____

EVIDENCE NOTEBOOK Research evidence that might explain some of the benefits and drawbacks of urbanization. Enter your findings in your Evidence Notebook.

Putting It Together

23. Write the correct answer for each sentence on the line.

> more   less   homes   trees

More people living on Earth means _____ resources

are used. Some effects of a growing human population include

deforestation, which involves removing all the _____

in an area.

A Solution for All This Pollution!

Explore Online

You use water every day for washing, cooking, bathing, and drinking. The water you drink is cleaned and treated at a water treatment plant. But what about the water you pour down the sink or flush down the toilet? How do sewage treatment plants filter and clean our waste water?

Objective

Collaborate to design your own method for filtering dirty water.

What question will you investigate to meet this objective?

_____

_____

_____

Materials

- beaker of dirty water
- 2 small graduated cylinders
- piece of wire screen
- coffee filters
- large gravel
- funnel
- potting soil
- large jar
- sand
- small pebbles

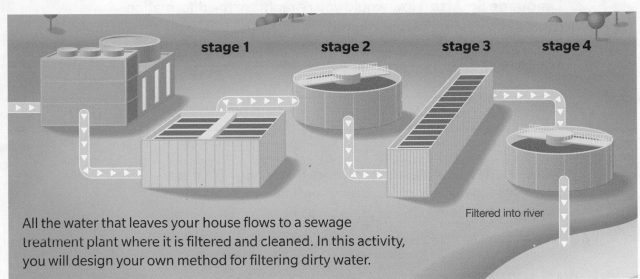

stage 1   stage 2   stage 3   stage 4

Filtered into river

All the water that leaves your house flows to a sewage treatment plant where it is filtered and cleaned. In this activity, you will design your own method for filtering dirty water.

Stage 1: Screening Screening removes large objects, such as plastics, rags, or cotton, that may block or damage equipment.

Stage 2: Primary treatment This stage removes organic solid matter from the wastewater. It is removed by putting the wastewater into large settlement tanks. Here the solids are scraped, pushed to the center of the tank, and pumped away.

Stage 3: Secondary treatment The wastewater is put into large rectangular tanks. Air is then pumped into it so bacteria can breakdown any leftover residue.

Stage 4: Final treatment The wastewater is now almost treated. It is passed through a settlement tank. Any leftover residue is scraped, and collected for treatment. The water will flow over a wall where it is filtered through a bed of sand. Finally, the filtered water is released into the river.

Procedure

STEP 1 Look over the materials. Get a beaker of dirty water from your teacher and two graduated cylinders. Pour some dirty water from the beaker into one of the graduated cylinders. Do not drink the water at any time.

STEP 2 Think about the materials that were provided to you and decide on a method for filtering the dirty water that is in the beaker. Formulate a hypothesis about how clean your water will be after filtering it. A hypothesis is a prediction or educated guess about what will happen in an investigation.

Enter your hypothesis on the lines below.

_____

_____

STEP 3 A hypothesis is testable. Plan the steps you will use to test your hypothesis.

List the steps below.

_____

_____

_____

_____

STEP 4 Clean the water using the method you chose and the steps you planned. Then, pour your filtered water into the other graduated cylinder.

461

STEP 5 Compare your filtered water with the dirty water. Record your observations in the Observations Table.

Observations	
Graduated cylinder with unfiltered water	**Graduated cylinder with filtered water**

Analyze Your Results

STEP 6 How did the filtered water compare to the dirty water?

_____

_____

STEP 7 Share your results with those from another group. How were they similar and different?

_____

_____

STEP 8 Do you think the filter cleaned the water? What can be in the water that the filter did not remove?

_____

_____

Draw Conclusions

STEP 9 Make a claim about your hypothesis. Cite evidence to support it.

_____

_____

STEP 10 How could I redesign my filtering method to make it more effective?

_____

_____

462

Discover More

463

Check out this path . . . or go online to choose one of these other paths.

Careers in
Science &
Engineering

• Sustainable Forests
• Overfishing

Marine Biologist

There are many careers that involve studying changes in the environment and Earth's natural resources. One of these careers is marine biology.

Marine biologists study organisms that live in the ocean. They explore how marine organisms and their environment affect each other. Sometimes, they also study ways that human activities, such as dumping pollutants into the oceans, affect ocean environments. At other times, they may offer solutions to some of the problems facing marine life. For example, they may suggest using sunken ships to replace declining coral populations.

24. Suppose you are a marine biologist. You have been given an assignment to research how the Southeast Florida Coral Reefs are being threatened. Record your findings below.

_____

_____

_____

25. As a marine biologist, what can you do to prevent Southeast Florida Coral Reefs from being threatened?

_____

_____

_____

Ecologist

Ecology studies the relationships between living organisms and their physical environment. Ecologists often have to study and explain how human actions affect other living things and their environment.

Rachel Carson (May 27, 1907–April 14, 1964) was an American ecologist and writer whose book, *Silent Spring*, helped raise awareness about the effects of pesticides and the issue of environmental pollution. The book was first published in 1962 and led to a ban on a harmful chemical known as DDT.

26. What areas of interest do you think Rachel Carson had?

_____

_____

Work as a team to research a program that helps restore wetlands. Evaluate the program. What does it do? How well is it working? What evidence supports your claims? Use your research to complete the table below.

Claims	Evidence

27. What would you change to make the program better? Write your recommendations on the lines below, then share them with the class.

_____

_____

_____

Lesson Check

Name _____

Can You Explain It?

1. Now that you've learned more about natural resources and the ways that human activities affect those resources, describe some ways that Las Vegas can protect its resources in the future. Be sure to do the following:

   • Tell about the resources people use every day.

   • Tell about how these resources can be conserved.

▷ Explore Online

EVIDENCE NOTEBOOK Use the information you've collected in your Evidence Notebook to help you cover each point above.

_____

_____

_____

_____

_____

Checkpoints

2. Which of the following are examples of pollution? Circle all that apply.

   a. Oil leaks from a tanker ship that ran aground on a reef.

   b. Soil is being used by humans for growing food.

   c. Acidic water leaks from a mine into a nearby wetland.

   d. A net breaks away from a fishing boat and drifts along the ocean floor, catching fish and other organisms.

3. Write the correct answer to complete each sentence.

renewable	nonrenewable	geosphere	hydrosphere
atmosphere	systems	precipitation	

Cooking food in a solar oven uses a _____ source of energy. Cooking

food in a microwave oven that runs on electricity produced by a coal-fired

energy station uses a _____ source of energy.

Water that evaporates from the oceans moves between two of Earth's systems—

the _____ and the atmosphere. Littering causes pollution of the

geosphere, and potentially all of Earth's _____.

4. Which of the following human impacts are more likely because of human
population growth? Circle all that apply.
a. Ships, trucks, and other vehicles that
transport oil are involved in accidents
that result in oil spills.

b. People cut down or burn areas of rain
forest to harvest wood and clear land
for growing sugarcane.

c. A city grows in size, with more roads,
more cars, and more smog.

d. Fishing boats harvest fish and other
marine organisms faster than those
populations can be replaced.

5. Which solution matches the environmental problem of vehicle emissions?
a. recycling programs   **c.** hybrid or electric cars
b. healthy farming methods   **d.** community farms

6. Many cities are growing rapidly. What are some solutions to this
environmental problem? Circle all that apply.
a. constructing more buildings
b. recycling programs
c. community farms
d. city transportation

Lesson Roundup

A. Which of the following are true about fossil fuels? Select all that apply.

a. They are renewable resources.

b. Their supplies are limited.

c. They are only found in the hydrosphere.

d. They can pollute air when they are burned.

e. They can be used to generate electricity.

B. Choose the correct answer for each sentence.

| renewable | nonrenewable | oil | natural gas | sunlight |

Coal is a _____ resource. To help reduce pollution from burning fossil

fuels, people can use _____ as an energy source.

C. Select the best answer for the question. What is one of the biggest challenges of solving the space debris problem?

a. finding out where the space debris is

b. knowing how many pieces of space debris there are

c. having enough fuel to gather the space debris

d. figuring out what to do with the debris once it's gathered

D. Choose the best answer for each sentence.

| biosphere | geosphere | hydrosphere |

When the Deepwater Horizon oil spill occurred, oil from the _____

leaked into the _____ and destroyed organisms in the

_____.

E. How has the growth of human population in the last 100 years affected Earth?

_____

_____

How Can People Protect the Environment?

This city uses solar energy to supply some of its energy. How do you think that might help the environment?

By the end of this lesson . . .
you'll be able to identify and explain many ways that people can help protect the environment.

468

Can You Explain It?

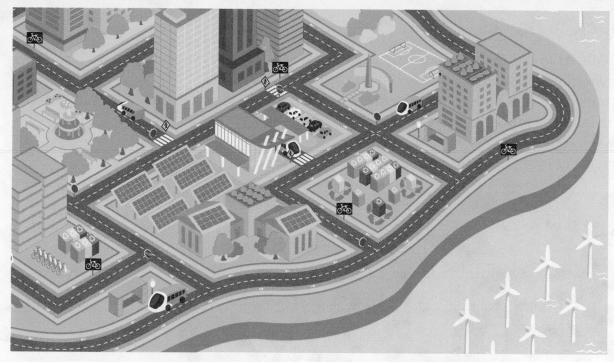

Look at the image showing a "green" city—a city that uses energy and resources efficiently and cleanly to minimize negative impacts on the environment.

1. What are some of the ways this city is helping the environment?

_____

_____

_____

_____

_____

_____

_____

_____

_____

Tip

Learn more about Earth's resources and how they affect the environment in How Does Resource Use Affect Earth?

 EVIDENCE NOTEBOOK Look for this icon to help you gather evidence to answer the question above.

What Are the Three Rs?

Back to Basics

You have already read about some of the ways that humans affect the environment. But there are many human activities that are helping to protect the environment. One group of these activities is known as the "three Rs"—reduce, reuse, recycle. The U.S. Environmental Protection Agency (EPA) has a priority approach to waste. First reduce, then reuse, and lastly, recycle.

When we **recycle,** we help make something new from used or broken items. This can involve breaking the item down to its raw ingredients. Although food scraps can make rich fertilizers or biofuels, they don't go in regular recycling bins. Read below to learn about the different items that can be recycled.

a. PET (polyethylene terephthalate) plastic is used to make drinking bottles.

b. Paper products range from milk cartons to newspapers.

c. Soda cans, food cans, and aluminum foil/ containers are made of metals.

d. Glass containers for food and liquids can be clear, brown, or green.

e. Polystyrene foam containers are not usually recyclable unless carefully cleaned.

f. Some areas have food waste recycling collection services where you can dispose your food scraps.

2. Why do you think it's important to clean some items before they are recycled?

Now let's take a closer look at some of these recyclable items. Read through each description to learn more.

More than 1.5 million barrels of oil are used to make plastic water bottles each year. It takes 400 years for a plastic bottle to **decompose,** or break down into simpler substances. Recycling helps conserve fossil fuels.

Paper or cardboard items are used by people every day. In fact, many of the paper items you use are probably made from recycled paper or cardboard. In the United States, almost 63% of all the paper products used are recycled.

Metal containers and aluminum foil can be melted down and used over and over again. Recycling food cans helps conserve fossil fuels, too. It also saves three-fourths of the energy needed to make new cans from raw metal.

Not all glass can be recycled, but brown, green, and clear glass can. Most glass containers made in this country are at least one-fourth recycled glass. Recycling glass conserves sand and the fossil fuels used in their production.

3. What are some recyclable items that you use every day? How does recycling help the environment?

_____

_____

_____

Using Less

One way to help the environment and its resources is to **reduce** your use of materials. When you reduce your use of an item, you make the size, number, or amount of that item smaller. Packaging produces a lot of waste that often ends up in landfills—structures built into or on top of the ground in which trash is isolated from the groundwater and air. Landfill waste stays in the landfill, where some of it decomposes. Unfortunately, many landfills leak harmful substances into the ground, are not built safely, or are full.

4. Look at each of the products below. Circle the items that are the best for helping to reduce waste.

a.

c.

b.

d.

5. Describe one item that you or your family uses that could be replaced by a larger version that has less packaging.

_____

_____

6. What are two things you can do to help reduce the amount of trash that ends up in landfills?

_____

_____

_____

One Person's Trash . . .

"One man's trash is another man's treasure." This would be a good slogan for another of the "three Rs": reuse. To **reuse** something simply means to use it again. You can prevent many items from ending up in landfills and avoid having to recycle them by finding ways to reuse them. Give clothes to charity. Use some cardboard and paper again. Wash glass bottles and jars.

7. Name three items that you regularly reuse in your daily life.

_____

_____

_____

Many community groups use tractor tires as climbing structures or swings in their playground areas.

Empty plastic bottles can be used to sprout seeds and grow plants. The bottles protect the plants and help them grow straight.

Food cans can be cleaned and decorated to be used as pen and pencil holders, craft supply containers, or brush holders.

Many recyclable materials can be used to create beautiful sculptures or other three-dimensional art pieces.

Many surfaces, such as this outdoor basketball court, are made with rubberized asphalt concrete. Tires are broken down and mixed with other materials to make the surfaces.

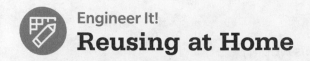

Reusing at Home

Take a walk around your house and observe the different items and materials. Are any of these items reusable?

8. Choose one item or material from your home, and engineer it so that it meets a certain need. Make sure you have permission to use that particular item. Write a description of the item and its new use, then make a labeled drawing of the item before and after engineering it. Submit your finished product, labeled drawing, and description to your teacher.

9. Complete the chart by filling in how each item can be reused. In the bottom row, enter another reusable item and an example of how it can be reused.

Item	How can it be reused?
Empty water bottles	
Clothing item you no longer use	
Cardboard box	
Gift wrapping	

10. How do the reuse ideas in the chart help the environment?

_____

_____

_____

_____

_____

Why Recycle?

Recycling conserves natural resources, protects the environment, and reduces the amount of waste that goes into landfills. This means less litter, fewer metals mined, fewer trees cut down, fewer habitats damaged, less energy used, and more resources conserved.

Paper goes through a process when it is being recycled. Read to find out more.

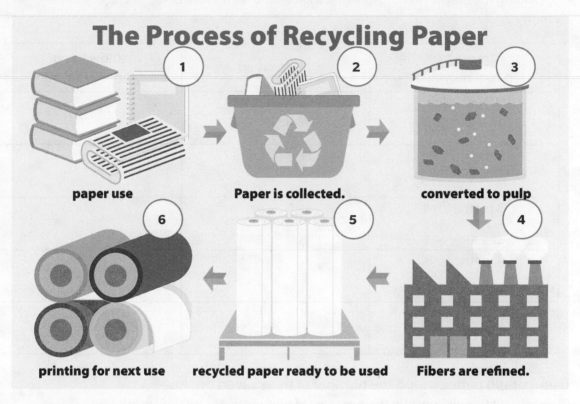

The Process of Recycling Paper

1 — paper use
2 — Paper is collected.
3 — converted to pulp
4 — Fibers are refined.
5 — recycled paper ready to be used
6 — printing for next use

Step 1: Paper use: Paper is used to make books, newspapers, and notebooks.

Step 2: Transportation: The recycled paper is collected and moved to processing facilities.

Step 3: Soaking and De-Inking: The paper soaks in vats, or large tanks, and becomes pulp; chemicals remove the ink.

Step 4: Screening and refining: Dirt, glue, and remaining ink are removed, and fibers refined.

Step 5: Sheeting and Rolling: The pulp is made into sheets that are rolled and dried.

Step 6: Used Again: The recycled paper is sold to companies to be reused.

11. How does recycling paper help the environment?

_____

_____

12. What is true of recycled paper?
   a. Paper can only be recycled once.
   b. Paper can be recycled many times.
   c. Recycled paper is usually sold as pulp.
   d. Recycled paper is expensive.

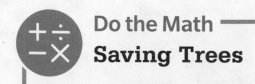

Do the Math
Saving Trees

13. Complete the table by filling in the correct numbers of trees and kilowatts of energy saved when recycling paper. Also, fill in the amount of paper recycled. Use the completed first row to figure out the correct numbers to place in the empty boxes. Note that a kilowatt is a measure of electrical energy.

Amount of paper recycled	Trees saved	Kilowatts of energy saved
1 metric ton (1,000 kilograms)	17	4,000
2 metric tons (2,000 kilograms)		8,000
3 metric tons _____		
4 metric tons _____		
5 metric tons _____		

Using graph paper, graph the number of trees saved on the horizontal axis (x-axis) versus the amount of kilowatts of energy saved on the vertical axis (y-axis) to show the relationship between the two variables. Submit your finished graph to your teacher.

14. Suppose a logging company wants to cut down 102 trees in your town to produce pulp for paper. What kind of conservation argument could you make against this proposal? Be sure to include specific numbers of energy saved based on the 102-tree target of the logging company.

_____

_____

_____

_____

_____

Recyclables in the Room

15. Look around the classroom to find items that can be recycled. Make a list of each recyclable item you located. Discuss your choices as a class. Talk about how each item can be reused and how reusing that item can help the environment.

As you have learned, recycling reduces our use of natural resources, helps reduce pollution, produces new jobs, and puts less waste in landfills. You have also learned about some common materials that are recyclable. Just as some material can be recycled, other objects can be made from that recycled material.

16. In the space provided below, draw a picture of an item that has been made from recycled materials. Write the name of this item, what materials it is made out of, and a sentence of how recycling this item helps the environment.

17. What items or products do you think can be made with recycled material but cannot be recycled? Explain your answer.

_____

_____

Recycled or Not?

Many things we use in our daily life are made from recycled items. A brown paper grocery bag can be made from recycled cardboard, newspaper, or office paper. Look at the items below. Do you think they're all made of recycled items? Read the captions to find out.

Some bicycles are made from aluminum cans. There's even a bicycle made from cardboard!

There are several backpacks on the market that are made from recycled plastic water bottles.

Doormats can be made from recycled rubber sandals and recycled plastic water bottles.

Children's toys and play sets can be made from different recycled plastics.

Some musical instruments can be made from recycled water bottles, wood products, and other recycled items.

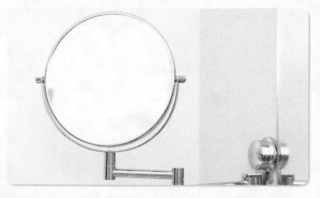

A mirror can be made from recycled glass. The backing of a mirror can be made from recycled recycled material, too. Mirrors are difficult to recycle though.

18. Would you be more likely to buy an item if you knew it was made from recycled materials? Why or why not?

19. In the box below each item, write the letter of the recycled material that it is made from. Some items are made of more than one material.

a. plastic bottle   **b.** metal can   **c.** cardboard   **d.** newspaper   **e.** office paper   **f.** plastic detergent bottles

Backpack	Bicycle
Musical instruments	**Doormat**
Brown paper grocery bags	**Plastic toy**

 EVIDENCE NOTEBOOK Gather evidence that explains how people who reduce, reuse, and recycle are helping to protect the environment. Enter the evidence in your Evidence Notebook.

 Language SmArts
Informative Paragraph

20. Choose the correct words to complete each sentence.

| landfills | mines | reduced | recycled |

Instead of throwing items away in _____ , many

items can be reused, recycled, or _____ . The

_____ materials can be used to make new products.

Tip

The English Language Arts Handbook can provide help with understanding how to write informative paragraphs.

Going Green

Innovative Green Technologies

People and businesses everywhere are "going green" by finding ways to protect the environment. Using renewable resources, recycling, and buying and selling products made from recycled materials are helping the planet. People are using products that are **biodegradable,** or break down naturally. Also, cities are incorporating "green" technologies to help the environment. Read below to learn more.

A Singapore theme park features a giant Supertree Grove. Each tree is made of ferns, orchids, and other plants and has solar cells that help provide energy for the entire park. Each tree has a collection area within where it collects rainwater to be used for irrigation and fountains.

The porous pattern on the outside of this building is made of a smog-eating material. The material breaks down air pollution when it is exposed to sunlight.

Cities around the globe are installing green walls. Green walls are building surfaces entirely covered with plant life. The plants provide shade, reduce noise, and remove pollutants from the air.

21. Conduct your own research to find out what kinds of green technologies are used in your community.

Paper or Plastic Bag Debate

Have you ever gone to the grocery store with your parents and heard the checkout clerk ask, "Paper or plastic?" What do you think the difference is between using paper or plastic bags? What are the advantages to using paper bags? What are the advantages to using plastic bags?

Prepare to debate the question, *Which is more environmentally friendy—paper bags or plastic bags?* Research the pros and cons of each. Decide which one most benefits the environment.

22. Use the table to record your claim about plastic and paper bags. Enter at least three pieces of evidence to support your claim.

Claim	Supporting evidence

23. Which do you think is the best type of bag for the environment? Why?

_____

_____

 24. Language SmArts Think about alternatives to using just paper and plastic bags. What options are there? What are the advantages and disadvantages? How can these alternatives help protect the environment?

_____

_____

Conserving at Home

There are many things you can do at home to conserve natural resources and help protect the environment. Look at the picture below. Try to see if you can find ways how energy can be conserved in this room. Then, read below to learn how you can bring conservation to your own bedroom.

A Conservation Game Plan

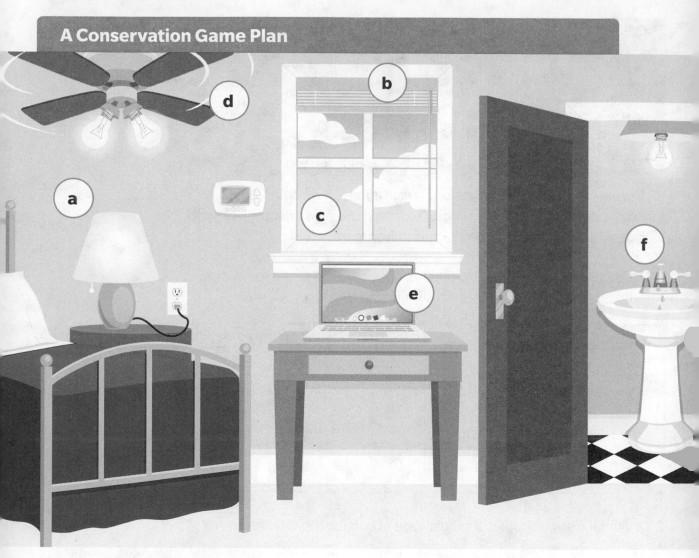

a. If your lights are on, you are using energy. Turn out the lights when they aren't needed.

b. Use your window blinds to regulate the temperature in the room. Sunlight produces heat, so the more open you keep your blinds, the more sunlight can get in and produce heat.

c. To save on cooling costs, keep windows closed during the hottest part of the day. Open up windows in the early morning and evening to let cool air in.

d. Use electric appliances, such as ceiling fans, only when you're in the room and really need them.

e. Check the settings on your computer so that when not in use, the sleep mode is activated.

f. To help conserve water, always turn the faucet off when you're not using the water. When brushing your teeth, only use enough water to wet your toothbrush and rinse.

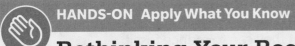

Rethinking Your Room

Think about your favorite room in your house. Is there anything you can do to make it more environmentally friendly?

25. Draw a diagram of your favorite room, and label all the ways you can help conserve energy there. Also, label each of the electric devices in the room, and identify whether it uses renewable or nonrenewable energy. Draw your diagram below, and submit it to your teacher.

26. Defend your choices. How do they help conserve energy?

_____

_____

_____

_____

Green Cities

Many cities around the country are doing what they can to reduce fossil fuel use, recycle, and improve energy efficiency, which involves using less energy to get the same amount of work or service from a product.

Cities Go Green

Cities around the world have found creative ways to help the environment. Look at each image, and read each caption to learn more about what cities are doing to reduce fossil fuels.

Discovery Green in Houston, Texas has trees, a lake, and a variety of wildlife. The park uses renewable sources for its energy and was built with environmentally friendly materials.

Some transit systems run on clean energy fuels, others do not. Many city transit systems are now offering a clean and safe way to get around, from buses to rail cars to electric vehicles. The more people use these options, the less they use fossil fuels.

Designated paths and lanes on roads provide bicycle enthusiasts with safe transportation options. People can also borrow or rent bikes.

Green rooftops help cool the air as well as remove carbon dioxide and pollutants. This makes the air safer to breathe.

Extensive recycling programs in many cities provide recycling bins and a reliable collection service to all city businesses and residents.

Many big cities are installing wind turbines and solar panel arrays to increase their use of renewable energy sources.

27. Research in books or on the Internet other ways a green city can help the environment. What did you learn?

_____

_____

28. Compare green cities to traditional cities. How do you think green cities can help protect the environment?

_____

_____

 EVIDENCE NOTEBOOK Gather evidence about more green technologies and green cities and how they are helping the environment. Write your findings in your Evidence Notebook.

Putting It Together

29. Choose the correct words to complete each sentence.

renewable	nonrenewable	cool	warm

Green technologies help the environment by developing ways to use more _____ energy sources. Green cities may feature green walls that help _____ and clean the air.

Pocket Park

Cities build these mini-parks to help increase the green space in the busy city environment. Cities throughout the United States and in other parts of the world are building pocket parks. Pocket parks are small green spaces that help the environment.

Materials
• pencil, pen, or markers
• copy paper
• graph paper 1/4" scale
• ruler

Objective

Collaborate to learn how pocket parks can help the environment.

FIND A PROBLEM: What question will you investigate to meet this objective?

_____

_____

Gather Information

Research: Research in books or online to find out what pocket parks and community gardens are, what their purpose is, and what features they include. Write your findings below.

_____

_____

_____

_____

Scenario: The members of Busyville have organized a community group. They are asking the city to provide them with a pocket park and community garden—a park space where their children can play and people living in the immediate area can interact or relax, and a garden where the community can plant and grow produce.

Problem

You and your team of engineers have been hired and given the task of designing a pocket park with a community garden. The park is going to be located in the middle of a vacant lot on Busyville's Action Avenue.

Make sure your pocket park and garden plans meet the following criteria and constraints.

Criteria	Constraints
☐ Your design should include features that help protect the environment.	☐ You must stay within your budget of 10,000 bookles. See the list below that gives specific prices for things such as planting trees and constructing a garden.
☐ The park should have space where children can play and where adults can interact or just relax.	☐ You have a space of 30x30 fazers, to build your pocket park. 1 square = 1 fazer
☐ The park should be visible from the street and accessible by foot and bicycle.	☐ The community garden should have the dimensions of 8x8 fazers. 1 square = 1 fazer

Pocket Park Per-Item Prices:

Garden construction—15 bookles per fazer
Trees—100 bookles per fazer
Playground construction—60 bookles per fazer
Trash bin—50 bookles per fazer
Compost bin—50 bookles per fazer
Recycling bin—25 bookles per fazer
Grass—20 bookles per fazer

Solar charging station—100 bookles per 2 fazers
Solar-powered water fountain (recycled and filtered water)—1,000 bookles per 5 fazers
Climbing wall and green wall—1,000 bookles per 5 fazers
Recycled benches—75 bookles per 3 fazers
Solar-powered light—50 bookles per fazer
Rubber mulch—5 bookles per fazer

Procedure

STEP 1 Research: Gather information and research to help you design the Busyville Pocket Park and Community Garden.

STEP 2 Brainstorm: With other students, come up with different ideas about how your pocket park should look, what features it will have, and where the features will go.

Define the problem in this activity. How can you design a pocket park to meet the community's needs?

STEP 3 Plan: Now it's time to start sketching. Make a couple of different sketches. Each sketch should show the dimensions of the pocket park, where the community garden will go, and where each of the features in the park will go. Choose the sketch you like best. Make a final diagram to present to the Busyville Planning Committee.

STEP 4 Communicate: Present your diagram to the Busyville Planning Committee—your classmates. Use their feedback to make any necessary improvements to your pocket park diagram.

What recommendations from your classmates are you going to use?

_____

_____

_____

STEP 5 Build: Make a final diagram of your Busyville Pocket Park and Community Garden. Include a scale in your drawing.

STEP 6 Use the table to keep track of the features in your pocket park, the amount of each feature needed, and the cost.

Feature	Amount needed	Cost
Totals		

Check over your final diagram showing your labeled Busyville Pocket Park and Community Garden. Double-check your table to make sure all features in the park are included. Submit your final diagram to your teacher.

Analyze Your Results

STEP 7 Evaluate: Does your pocket park plan meet all the constraints and criteria? If not, explain.

_____

_____

_____

_____

STEP 8 How many sketches did you make? Which sketch did you choose as the final plan for your pocket park and garden? Why?

_____

_____

_____

_____

STEP 9 What features did you include in your pocket park?

_____

_____

_____

STEP 10 Which features in your park and garden are environmentally friendly?

_____

_____

_____

_____

_____

_____

_____

Draw Conclusions

STEP 11 Make a claim about how pocket parks and community gardens help protect the environment. Cite evidence to support your claim

_____

_____

_____

STEP 12 What did you learn from planning this pocket park and garden?

_____

_____

_____

STEP 13 What improvements could you make to your Busyville Pocket Park and Community Garden plan?

_____

_____

_____

Discover More

Check out this path.. . . or go online to choose one of these other paths.

People in
Science &
Engineering

• **Landfills: How Long Until It's Gone?**
• **Can All Plastics Be Recycled?**

Boyan Slat

Boyan Slat is a twenty-year-old Netherlands engineering student whose Ocean Cleanup plan offers solutions to the ocean trash problem.

Boyan Slat first became interested in removing plastic trash from the ocean when he was diving in Greece and discovered there were more plastic bags in the water than there were fish.

Here are ocean pollution facts:

• Each year, 8 million tons of plastic go into the oceans.

• About 5.25 trillion plastic items are now floating in the ocean.

• Plastic pollution kills about 1 million seabirds annually.

• Plastic pollution kills about 100,000 sea mammals annually.

30. Write one additional ocean pollution fact by doing research online.

_____

_____

31. How can we prevent plastic from getting into the ocean?

_____

_____

491

Plastic Pollution Solution

There are many areas of concentrated debris in the ocean. The most well known is found in the Pacific Ocean and is called the Great Pacific Garbage Patch. These trash patches form when winds and currents in the ocean cause floating debris, such as plastic bags, tiny bits of plastic, and other pieces of trash, to swirl together in circular currents called gyres. Boyan Slat developed a solution called Ocean Cleanup. This project is still in the pilot phase.

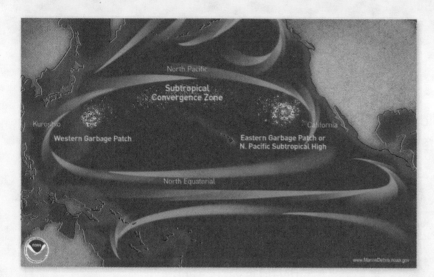

About 30 percent of the plastic in the ocean accumulates in the Great Pacific Garbage Patch.

Boyan Slat's Ocean Cleanup solution uses a system, or array, of floating barriers that collects the plastic debris in the ocean.

One array of floating barriers has the ability to clean half the Great Pacific Garbage Patch in 10 years.

32. How do you think trash in the ocean affects the animals that live there?

_____

_____

_____

33. If you could ask Boyan Slat a question, what would it be?

_____

_____

Lesson Check

Name _____

Can You Explain It?

1. Now that you've learned more about protecting the environment, describe how this green city is protecting the environment. Be sure to do the following:

   • Identify each example that shows how the green city is protecting the environment.

   • Explain how each example protects the environment.

   • List some other ways the green city can protect the environment.

EVIDENCE NOTEBOOK Use the information you collected in your Evidence Notebook to help you cover each point above.

_____

_____

_____

_____

_____

_____

_____

_____

Checkpoints

2. A family wants to move to a green city. Which features of the city would they find more appealing? Circle the correct answer.

   a. a city that replaced one of its parks with apartments

   b. a city that is building two new landfills outside of town

   c. a city with a large community garden and a recycling program

   d. a city with a natural gas power plant and a coal power plant

3. How are "green cities" finding ways to help protect the environment? Circle all that apply.

    a. By using more renewable energy sources.

    b. By using more nonrenewable energy sources.

    c. By establishing extensive recycling programs.

    d. By offering transit systems that run on clean energy.

4. Choose the words that correctly complete the sentences.

| **batteries** | **plastics** | **only clear glass** | **most glass** | **only colored glass** |

Paper products, _____, and glass bottles are examples of

items that can go into a regular recycling bin. When recycling glass bottles,

remember that _____ bottles can be recycled.

5. Which of the following are examples of someone practicing at least two of the "three Rs"? Circle all that apply.

    a. After using a zip-top plastic bag to store a loaf of bread, James realizes he can also use the bag to hold a bottle of sunblock and a small tube of toothpaste in his luggage for his trip.

    b. Grant decides to install a water filter on the faucet of his kitchen sink instead of spending money on five-gallon bottles of spring water.

    c. Maria finishes using a bottle of water. She then cuts it into two halves to make small pots for growing tomato seeds. After transplanting the seedlings to a garden, she recycles the bottle halves.

    d. Hyun decides to "green" his restaurant by offering washable stainless steel chopsticks instead of disposable wooden chopsticks.

6. Circle all the actions you can take at home to help conserve energy.

    a. Throw clear glass away in the garbage.

    b. Turn off lights that aren't being used.

    c. Don't leave water running.

    d. Put newspapers in the recycling bin.

    e. Use rechargeable batteries and a solar charger.

    f. Throw paper products away in the garbage.

Lesson Roundup

A. What is a landfill? Circle all that apply.

   a. A place to dispose of waste material.

   b. A place where you can take your recycled items
   to be recycled.

   c. A food waste recycling collection service.

   d. A structure built into or on top of the ground
   where waste material is isolated from
   groundwater and air.

B. Circle all the ways that the number of small plastic water bottles can be reduced.

   a. Use them as planters.

   b. Put them in a Recycle bin.

   c. Use a filter to filter tap water.

   d. Buy a smaller number of larger
   bottles of water.

C. Keep track of anything else you learned about the three Rs, and write it here!

_____

_____

D. Choose the words that correctly complete the sentence.

| renewable | nonrenewable | environment | energy efficiency |

   The purpose of green technology is to keep _____ energy use at

a minimum and _____ energy use at a maximum. The main reason

many cities are "going green" is to find ways to protect our _____.

Cities are doing what they can to improve _____.

E. Write one thing you learned about green cities and green technologies.

_____

_____

_____

Protecting a Sphere

You are on a mission to find and tell others ways to protect the different spheres of the Earth. In small groups, you will work together to create a public service announcement about protecting a sphere of the Earth.

How many spheres are in this picture?

STEP 1: What do you want to accomplish with your public service announcement?

_____

_____

_____

Before beginning, look at the checklist at the end of this project to be sure you are meeting all the requirements.

STEP 2: Identify Earth's spheres as well as identify which sphere your group will create a public service announcement for.

_____

_____

_____

STEP 3: Brainstorm three or more ways to present your public service announcement. Keep in mind the criteria and constraints.

_____

_____

_____

_____

_____

STEP 4: Consider the form your public announcement will take.

a. What general concepts do you want to address?

b. What materials will you need for your public service announcement and how wil you use those materials?

Present a step-by-step plan here.

_____

_____

_____

_____

_____

_____

_____

_____

Brainstorm to decide how to present the public service announcement.

STEP 5: Does your presentation address the issues with your sphere? What are some ways you can improve the public service announcement?

_____

_____

_____

STEP 6: Present your public service announcement to the class.

☑ Checklist

Review your project and check off each completed item.

_____ Identifies the Earth's sphere in the public service announcement.

_____ Includes an explanation of the importance of protecting and conserving the sphere.

_____ Includes an explanation of what can happen if the sphere is not conserved.

_____ Includes an explanation of how conserving the sphere can be beneficial to organisms.

_____ Includes drawings to support points of conservation.

Unit Review

1. Look at the various types of resources in the images. Choose all of the renewable resources.

   a. natural gas

   b. wind

   c. oil

   d. water

   e. coal

   f. sun

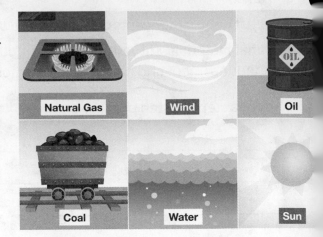

2. Compare the geosphere and hydrosphere by writing the words or phrases that affect each sphere, into the Venn diagram.

| building roads | overfishing | poor farming practices | littering |
| deforestation | pollution | ocean debris | construction |

Geosphere	Both	Hydrosphere

3. Select the best description of a population.

   a. plants and animals that inhabit Earth's many spheres

   b. a species that has the greatest impact on the environment

   c. all the organisms of the same kind that live together in a given area

   d. a varied group of species that represent different types of living things

4. There are pros and cons in building a dam. What is the solution to the environmental problem depicted in this image of a dam?

   a. Remove the dam and restore the surrounding habitats.

   b. Join a beach clean-up group.

   c. Participate in more recycling programs.

   d. Use public transportation more often.

   e. Use healthier farming methods.

5. A neighborhood is trying to protect as many of Earth's resources as they can by making small changes to their habits. Select all the changes they can make that will help protect Earth's resources.

   a. start community gardens

   b. start a plastic recycling program

   c. remove the trees and plant gardens

   d. reduce the amount of water in their local dam

   e. use fewer pesticides in the community garden

   f. use stronger fertilizer to make the plants grow bigger

   g. set up a car pool program to share the driving to places

6. Savannah is working on a class project to help her school "go green." After conducting surveys and obtaining information from the school, Savannah found that 75% of students are dropped off every morning by a parent, the school put recycling bins in every classroom, and the school participates in a water conservation program.

   Based on these findings, which of the following efforts does Savannah's school need to focus on **most** to be more "green"?

   a. Putting two or more recycle bins in each classroom

   b. Limiting the amount of water used by each student

   c. Trying to get more students to take the bus

   d. Convincing the school to buy solar panels for the roofs

7. Write the word to best complete the sentence.

> conserve   recycle   urbanize

Deforestation is a major problem, particularly for the Amazon rain

forests. Environmentalists are trying to _____ rain

forest plant and animal life.

8. What kind of environmental conservation effort is being depicted in the image?

a. reducing fossil fuels

b. using recycled water

c. reusing solar power

d. providing natural energy

9. Categorize the human activities into whether they have a positive or negative effect on the environment by writing the words or phrases into the correct column. Some items may appear in both columns.

- transit systems
- green walls
- dams
- recycle bins

Positive	Negative

10. Look at the picture of the landfill. How would the landfill be affected if everyone in the community reduced, reused, or recycled more?

a. More animal and plant life would be preserved.

b. The amount of waste would decrease.

c. Urbanization would be stopped.

d. Garbage would no longer exist.

Interactive Glossary

As you learn about each item, add notes, drawings, or sentences in the extra space. This will help you remember what the terms mean. Here is an example:

fungi (FUHN•jee) A group of organisms that get nutrients by decomposing other organisms

hongos Un grupo de organismos que obtienen sus nutrientes al descomponer otros organismos.

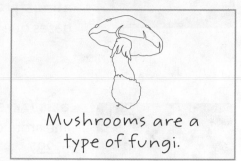

Mushrooms are a type of fungi.

Glossary Pronunciation Key

With every glossary term, there is also a phonetic respelling. A phonetic respelling writes the word the way it sounds, which can help you pronounce new or unfamiliar words. Use this key to help you understand the respellings.

Sound	As in	Phonetic Respelling	Sound	As in	Phonetic Respelling
a	bat	(BAT)	oh	over	(OH•ver)
ah	lock	(LAHK)	oo	pool	(POOL)
air	rare	(RAIR)	ow	out	(OWT)
ar	argue	(AR•gyoo)	oy	foil	(FOYL)
aw	law	(LAW)	s	cell	(SEL)
ay	face	(FAYS)		sit	(SIT)
ch	chapel	(CHAP•uhl)	sh	sheep	(SHEEP)
e	test	(TEST)	th	that	(THAT)
	metric	(MEH•trik)		thin	(THIN)
ee	eat	(EET)	u	pull	(PUL)
	feet	(FEET)	uh	medal	(MED•uhl)
	ski	(SKEE)		talent	(TAL•uhnt)
er	paper	(PAY•per)		pencil	(PEN•suhl)
	fern	(FERN)		onion	(UHN•yuhn)
eye	idea	(eye•DEE•uh)		playful	(PLAY•fuhl)
i	bit	(BIT)		dull	(DUHL)
ing	going	(GOH•ing)	y	yes	(YES)
k	card	(KARD)		ripe	(RYP)
	kite	(KYT)	z	bags	(BAGZ)
ngk	bank	(BANGK)	zh	treasure	(TREZH•er)

A

atmosphere (AT•muhs•feer) The mixture of gases that surround a planet. p. 368

atmósfera Combinación de los gases que rodean el planeta.

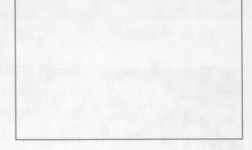

axis (AK•sis) The imaginary line around which Earth rotates. p. 297

eje Línea imaginaria en torno a la cual rota la Tierra.

B

biodegradable [by•oh•dee•GRA•duh•buhl] Able to be decomposed by living organisms. p. 480

biodegradable Que puede ser descompuesto por organismos vivos.

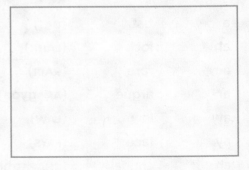

biosphere (BY•oh•sfeer) All the living things on Earth. p. 368

biósfera Conjunto de todos los seres vivos de la Tierra.

boiling point (BOYL•ing POINT) The point at which matter changes from a liquid to a gas. p. 132

punto de ebullición Punto en el que la materia cambia de líquido a gas.

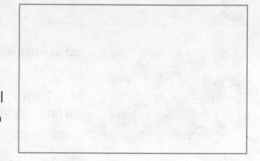

brainstorming (BRAYN•storm•ing) Collecting as many ideas as you can, however good you think they are. p. 32

lluvia de ideas Recopilación de la mayor cantidad de ideas posible, sin importar el valor que creas que puedan tener.

chemical change (KEM•ih•kuhl CHAYNJ) Change in one or more substance, caused by a reaction, that forms new and different substances. p. 136

cambio químico Cambio en una sustancia o más, causado por una reacción que genera sustancias nuevas y distintas.

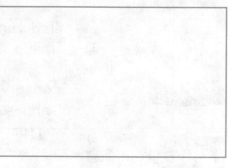

C

coastline (KOST•lyn) The place at which land masses meet the ocean. p. 420

costa Lugar en el que las masas terrestres se encuentran con el océano.

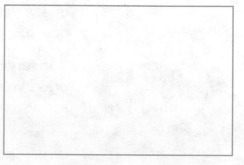

C

community
(kuh•MYOO•nih•tee) A group of organisms that live in the same area and interact with one another. p. 205

comunidad Grupo de organismos que viven en la misma área e interactúan entre sí.

condensation
(kahn•duhn•SAY•shuhn) The process by which a gas changes into a liquid. p. 391

condensación Proceso por el cual un gas se convierte en líquido.

conservation of matter
(kahn•ser•VAY•shuhn uhv MAT•ur) A law that states that matter cannot be made or destroyed; however, matter can change into a new form. p. 143

conservación de la materia Ley que establece que la materia no se crea ni se destruye, sino que se transforma en algo nuevo.

conserve (kuhn•SERV) To preserve and protect an ecosystem or a resource. p. 448

conservar Preservar y proteger un ecosistema o recurso.

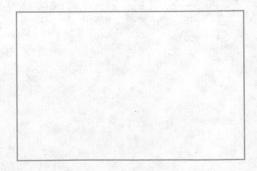

constellation
(kon•stuh•LEY•shuhn) A pattern of stars that form an imaginary picture or design in the sky. p. 296

constelación Patrón de estrellas que forman un diseño o dibujo imaginario en el cielo.

constraint (KUHN•straint) Something that limits the solution you are designing. p. 28

restricción Algo que limita la solución que se está diseñando.

consumer (kuhn•SOOM•er) A living thing that cannot make its own food and must eat other living things. p. 182

consumidor Ser vivo que no puede producir su propio alimento y por eso debe alimentarse de otros seres vivos.

criteria (kry•TEER•ee•uh) The desirable features of a solution. p. 28

criterios Características deseables para una solución.

D

decompose (dee•kuhm•POHZ) Breaking down dead organisms and animal wastes into simpler substances to get energy. p. 471

descomponer Romper, separar o desbaratar organismos muertos y desperdicios animales en sustancias más simples para obtener energía.

decomposer (dee•kuhm•POHZ•er) A living thing that gets energy by breaking down dead organisms and animal wastes into simpler substances. p. 227

descomponedor Ser vivo que obtiene su energía al romper, separar o desbaratar organismos muertos y

desperdicios animales en sustancias más simples.

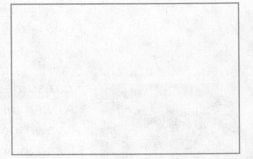

deforestation (de•FOR•is•ta•shuhn) The process of cutting down trees to plant crops. p. 41

deforestación Acción de cortar y eliminar árboles para el cultivo.

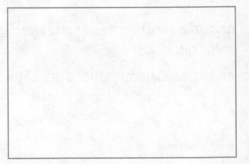

E

ecosystem (EE•koh•sis•tuhm) A community of organisms and the environment in which they live. p.198

ecosistema Comunidad de organismos y ambiente en el que viven.

energy pyramid (EN•er•jee PIR•uh•mid) A diagram that shows that energy is lost at each level in a food chain. p. 237

pirámide de energía Diagrama que muestra que se pierde energía en cada nivel de la cadena alimentaria.

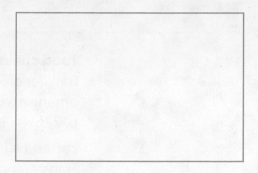

environment (en•VY•ruhn•muhnt) All of the living and nonliving things that surround and affect an organism. p. 198

medio ambiente Todo los seres vivos y no vivos que rodean y afectan a un organismo.

erosion (uh•ROH•zhuhn) The process of moving sediment from one place to another. p. 30

erosión Acción de mover sedimento de un lugar a otro.

evaporation (ee•VAP•uh•ray•shuhn) The process by which a liquid changes into a gas. p. 391

evaporación Proceso por el cual un líquido se transforma en gas.

food chain (FOOD CHAYN) The transfer of food energy between organisms in an ecosystem. p. 226

cadena alimentaria Transferencia de energía alimentaria entre organismos en un ecosistema.

food web (FOOD WEB) A group of food chains that overlap. p. 230

red alimentaria Grupo de cadenas alimentarias que se superponen.

freezing point (FREE•zing POINT) The temperature at which matter changes from a liquid to a solid. p. 130

punto de congelación Temperatura en la que la materia cambia de líquida a sólida.

geosphere (JEE•o•sfeer) The solid portion of Earth. p. 369

geósfera La parte sólida de la Tierra.

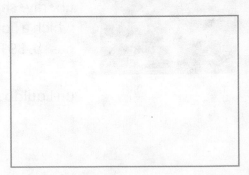

gravity (GRAV•ih•tee) A force that pulls things toward the center of the Earth. p. 283

gravedad Fuerza que atrae los objetos hacia el centro de la Tierra.

H

habitat (HAB•ih•tat) The place where an organism lives and can find everything it needs to survive. p. 200

hábitat Lugar donde vive un organismo y donde puede encontrar todo lo necesario para sobrevivir.

hemisphere (HEM•i•sfeer) One half of Earth. p. 284

hemisferio Una mitad de la Tierra.

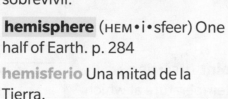

hydrosphere (HI•dro•sfeer) All of Earth's water, taken together in all states of matter. p. 369

hidrósfera Toda el agua de la Tierra, junta y en cualquier estado de la materia.

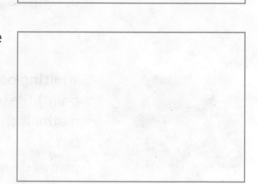

I

invasive species (in•VAY•siv SPEE•sheez) An organism that is nonnative to an environment and disrupts the stable web of life. p. 250

especies invasivas Organismo que no es nativo de un ambiente y altera la red estable de la vida.

M

matter (MAT•er) Anything that has mass and takes up space. p. 78

materia Cualquier cosa que tiene masa y ocupa espacio.

melting point (MEL•ting point) The temperature at which matter is changed from a solid p. 131

punto de fusión Temperatura en la cual la materia cambia de sólido a líquido.

mixture (MIKS•cher) A combination of two or more different substances in which the substances keep their identities. p. 114

mezcla Combinación de dos o más sustancias diferentes en la que estas mantienen sus identidades.

N

natural resource (NACH•er•uhl REE•sawrs) Anything from nature that people can use. p. 448

recurso natural Todo lo que provenga de la naturaleza y que las personas puedan usar.

niche (NICH) The role that a plant or animal plays in its habitat. p. 200

nicho Rol que juega una planta o un animal en su hábitat.

O

orbit (AWR•bit) The path of one object in space around another object. p. 314

órbita La trayectoria de un objeto alrededor de otro en el espacio.

P

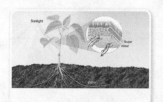

photosynthesis (foh•toh•SIN•thuh•sis) The process that plants use to make sugar. p.170

fotosíntesis Proceso en el cual las plantas generan azúcar.

P

physical change (FIZ•ih•kuhl CHAYNJ) A change in which the shape or form of the substance changes but the substance still has the same physical makeup. p. 128

cambio físico Transformación en la que cambia el estado o la forma de una sustancia pero esta se mantiene con la misma composición física.

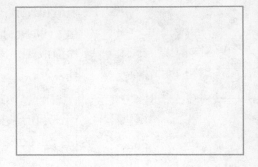

physical properties (FIZ•ih•kuhl PRAHP•er•tees) Anything that you can observe about an object by using one or more of your senses. p. 106

propiedad física Todo lo que se pueda observar de un objeto usando uno o más sentidos.

pollution (puh•LOO•shuhn) Any waste product or contamination that harms or dirties an ecosystem and harms organisms. p. 449

contaminación Todo desperdicio que daña o ensucia un ecosistema y hace daño a sus organismos.

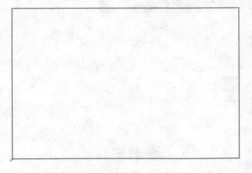

population (pahp•yuh•LAY•shuhn) All the organisms of the same kind that live together in a given area. pp. 205, 452

población Todos los organismos del mismo tipo que viven juntos en un ecosistema.

precipitation (pree•sip•uh•TAY•shuhn) Water that falls from the air to Earth's surface. p. 391

precipitación Agua que cae del aire a la superficie de la Tierra.

predator (PRED•uh•ter) An animal that hunts, catches, and eats other animals. p. 208

depredador Animal que caza, atrapa y come otros animales.

prey (PRAY) Animals that are caught and eaten by predators. p. 208

presa Animales que son atrapados y comidos por los depredadores.

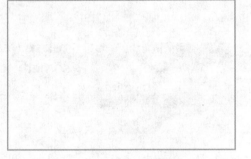

producer (pruh•DOOS•er) A living thing, such as a plant, that can make its own food. p. 182

productor Ser vivo, como las plantas, que es capaz de producir su propio alimento.

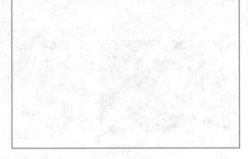

R

recycle (ree•SY•kuhl) To use the materials in old things to make new things. p. 470

reciclar Utilizar los materiales de cosas viejas para crear cosas nuevas.

reduce (ree•DOOS) To use less of something. p. 472

reducir Disminuir el uso de algo.

reuse (ree•YOOS) To use something again. p. 473

reutilizar Volver a usar algo.

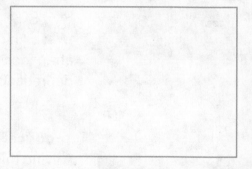

revolution (rev•uh•LOO•shuhn) The movement of Earth one time around the sun. p. 314

revolución Movimiento de la Tierra a lo largo de una órbita completa alrededor del Sol.

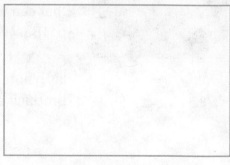

rotation (ro•TAY•shuhn) The turning of Earth on its axis. p. 297

rotación Giro de la Tierra sobre su propio eje.

S

scavenger (SKAV•in•jer) An animal that feeds on dead plants and animals. p. 227

carroñero Animal que se alimenta de plantas y animales muertos.

solution (suh•LOO•shuhn) A mixture that has the same composition throughout because all its parts are mixed evenly. p. 116

solución Mezcla que mantiene la misma composición a través de ella porque todas sus partes se han mezclado uniformemente.

S

system (SIS•tuhm) A set of connected things forming a complex whole. p. 368

sistema Conjunto de cosas conectadas entre sí que forman un todo complejo.

T

tradeoff (TRAID•awf) The process of giving up one quality or feature of a design to gain a different quality or feature.

intercambio Proceso de abandonar una cualidad o característica de un diseño para obtener una cualidad o característica diferente.

W

water cycle (WAW•ter SY•kuhl) The process in which water continuously moves from Earth's surface into the atmosphere and back again. p. 390

ciclo del agua Proceso en el que el agua se mueve continuamente desde la superficie terrestre hasta la atmósfera y de regreso.

Index

body repair, 183
boiling point, 131, 132
Bombelli, Paolo, 173–174
brainstorming, 32–33, 199, 330, 486–487
brass, 139
bread baking, 141, 142
breakwater, 423
briquettes, 80–81
Brown, Beth, 333
buoy, weather station, 407
burning, 136, 142, 147–148

C

CAD (computer assisted design), 63
calendar, 341, 353–354
Capella (star), 326, 327
carbon, 81–83
carbon cycle, 404–405
carbon dioxide, 170–172, 181–182, 247, 404
Careers in Science and Engineering
  animal nutritionist, 191–192
  astronomer, 306–308, 332
  astrophysicist, 333
  automotive engineers, 60–62, 63–64
  biochemist, 173–174
  climate scientist, 433
  designer, 173–174
  geologist, 434
  marine biologist, 463–464
  materials scientist, 95–96
  physician, 121–122
  physicist, 121
  plant scientist, 173–174
  safety engineer, 63
  software engineer, 21–22
  U.S. Army Corps of Engineers, 259–260
  volcanologist, 383–384
  zoologist, 239–240

cars
  air pollution from, 53, 60, 392–393, 449, 453
  design, 46–48, 56–59, 60–62
  fuel efficiency, 50–51, 60–61
  impacts of, 52–55, 453
  safety, 49, 60–61
  windshield strength, 64
Carson, Rachel, 464
centimeter, 93
Chandra X-ray Observatory, 333
charcoal, 80–81, 82
chemical changes, 136–142
  in burning, 136, 142
  in chemical reaction, 136
  in composting, 141
  conservation of matter in, 146, 147–148
  in cooking, 137, 140–141
  definition, 136
  in electroplating, 139
  physical changes and, 136
  in rotting, 136, 138
  in rusting, 138
cities, environmental impacts from, 248, 453
claim
  in *Hands-On Activity,* for example, 59, 169, 187, 234, 281
  in lessons, 92, 318, 353, 459, 464, 483
Cliffs of Moher (Ireland), 422
climate
  climate change, 428, 433, 449
  El Niño and La Niña, 426–427, 428
  ocean surface currents and, 424–425
  weather, 373, 402, 407–408
climate scientists, 433
clock, 301
clouds, 391, 397, 408
coal, 80–81, 448

coastal erosion, 423
comet, 316
community, 205–206, 381
composting, 141
computers
  computer assisted design, 63
  ecosystem simulations, 209–210
  saving energy in, 481–482
  software engineering, 21–22
condensation, 390–391, 398, 399
conductivity
  electrical, 110–111, 121
  semiconductors, 121
  thermal, 110–111
conductors, 110–111, 121
conservation of matter
  in chemical changes, 146, 147–148
  law of, 148
  in physical changes, 143–145
conservation of natural resources, 448, 481–482, 484
constellations, 296, 322–323, 339, 349–352
constraints
  definition, 28
  in engineering problems, 288, 450, 455
  in *Hands-On Activity;* 37, 56, 329–330, 487, 489
  identifying, 28, 29, 42–43
consumers, 182, 227, 229, 235–236
continental shelf, 417
contour lines, 29
cooking, chemical changes in, 137, 140–142
copper, 139
coral reef, 247, 428
corals, 428, 429
core, of Earth, 370
crane (equipment), 286